AF557792

Striving to promote and implement the preservation and conservation of the historic monuments and cultural heritage of the Deccan within a holistic environment and social context

Deccan Heritage Foundation Ltd
20–22 Bedford Row
London WC1R 4JS
www.deccanheritagefoundation.org

KAKATIYA HERITAGE TRUST
1-1-894 Siddharth Nagar,
REC Post, Warangal,
Telangana, 504004
www.kakatiyaheritage.org

DESIGN Nidhi Sah
PRINTING JAK Printers Pvt Ltd

ISBN 978-93-87944-85-5

First Jaico Impression 2018

PUBLISHED BY
Jaico Publishing House
A-2 Jash Chambers,
7-A Sir Phirozshah Mehta Road
Fort, Mumbai - 400 001
jaicopub@jaicobooks.com
www.jaicobooks.com

HERITAGE OF THE KAKATIYAS

Hanamkonda, Warangal, Palampet, Ghanpur

The Deccan Heritage Foundation would like to acknowledge the generous support of Shranutha Reddy and Arvind Bhaskar, and Jai and Sugandha Hiremath, in bringing out this publication

HERITAGE OF THE KAKATIYAS

Hanamkonda, Warangal, Palampet, Ghanpur

PHILLIP B. WAGONER

PHOTOGRAPHY Surendra Kumar

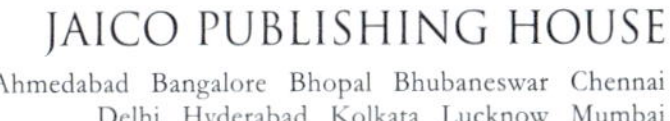

KAKATIYA HERITAGE TRUST

PREVIOUS PAGES

PAGE 1
Hanamkonda, Bhadrakali Lake
PAGE 3
Hanamkonda, Thousand-Pillared Temple, ceiling detail
PAGES 4 AND 5
Palampet, Ramappa Temple, female bracket figures

ABOVE Palampet, Ramappa Temple, carvings on ceiling beam showing Shiva dancing in the flayed skin of the elephant demon, flanked by other gods

FOLLOWING PAGES

PAGES 8 AND 9
Hanamkonda, Thousand-Pillared Temple, *jali* screens
PAGE 10
Hanamkonda, Thousand-Pillared Temple, priest in the Rudreshvara shrine

CONTENTS

FOREWORD

The Kakatiyas brought the Telugu speaking region of southern India under one political unit for around 300 years, leaving an indelible mark on cultural history that should be regarded as a golden period for this part of the Deccan. The magnificent temples of the Kakatiyas are unique in form as well as function, and in their time were not merely centres of worship but also repositories of political, social and cultural ethos. The sculptures are the epitome of the time for the knowledge and science displayed by Kakatiya art. Together with the inscriptions on the monuments, the sculptures are invaluable reserves, educating the populace about these aspects. Though many temples have been destroyed due to the invasions of the Delhi Sultanate, or have deteriorated over the centuries through structural collapse, their remains still communicate the glorious past of the Kakatiyas in Telangana.

The Kakatiya Heritage Trust is striving to preserve, protect and propagate the contribution made by the Kakatiyas. Since 2009, the Trust has been working on capacity building and heritage management of the Kakatiya historical sites by educating professionals and students about the rich heritage of Telangana, and bringing out several publications on Kakatiya legacy. In association with the Archaeological Survey of India and the Department of Heritage Telangana, the

Trust is working towards the nomination of the Ramappa temple at Palampet as a UNESCO World Heritage Site, the first in Telangana.

We are confident that this guidebook by Dr. Phillip B. Wagoner, along with the photographs of Surendra Kumar, will give the readers a unique insight into the splendid art and architecture of the Kakatiyas, and show the engineering marvels of the people of Telangana some 800 years ago. The author, who is Professor of Art History and Archaeology at Wesleyan University in Connecticut, has conducted extensive research on the cultural history of the Deccan over the past four decades, primarily focusing on the late medieval and early modern periods.

Hanamkonda, Warangal, Palampet, Ghanpur is a concise book explaining the history of Kakatiya historical sites, types of temples, city plans and irrigation projects, as well as the splendid art of the Kakatiyas. We are grateful to JAICO and the Deccan Heritage Foundation for co-publishing this guidebook under the expert editorial guidance of Dr. George Michell.

B.V. Papa Rao, IAS (Retired)
Trustee, Kakatiya Heritage Trust

Prof. M. Pandu Ranga Rao
Trustee, Kakatiya Heritage Trust

AUTHOR'S PREFACE

From the late 12th century through the early 14th century, the city of Warangal was the seat of the Kakatiya kingdom that held sway over the entire Telugu speaking area. The Kakatiya period was a time of rapid agricultural development and considerable prosperity in this part of the Deccan, as well as of notable achievements in literature, dance, and art. Temples were built throughout the Telangana region, often in conjunction with the construction of vast water reservoirs that still serve the needs of farmers. It is one of the great ironies that even the most important of these stunning architectural achievements remain so poorly known today. This guidebook aims to inspire travellers to visit these monuments, and to that end it offers essential information about the temples and other historical monuments of Kakatiya Telangana, illustrated with splendid, specially commissioned photographs by Surendra Kumar.

Although examples of Kakatiya architecture may be seen in virtually every district of Telangana State, this guidebook focuses on just four sites: Hanamkonda and Warangal (Warangal Urban District), which were the successive capitals of the Kakatiya kingdom; and Palampet and Ghanpur (in Jayashankar Bhupalpalli District), both with temples patronized by the Recherlas, one of the Kakatiyas' most prominent feudatory families. This somewhat narrow focus has been taken for two reasons. First, these four sites contain some of the most important Kakatiya monuments in all of Telangana, with examples of architecture that should be at the top of anyone's "to visit" list. Second, they are all readily accessible, Hanamkonda and Warangal being just a three-hour drive from Hyderabad, and Palampet and Ghanpur a little more than one hour beyond Warangal. There are of course other significant Kakatiya monuments in other parts of Telangana, but these are only rarely grouped in readily accessible clusters such as those included here.

The author first became familiar with Kakatiya architecture in 1982, spending a year and a half carrying out field documentation at some 27 sites across the region of Telangana (then part of northern Andhra Pradesh). He returned to the region in 1999 and again in 2005, these times focusing on the post-Kakatiya monuments of Warangal. Given this long-standing interest in Kakatiya Telangana, he was delighted when the Deccan Heritage Foundation and the Kakatiya Heritage Trust invited him to author this guidebook. He is most grateful to B.V. Papa Rao, Helen Philon, and George Michell for the commission, and also to the Foundation and the Trust for enabling him to visit the monuments again in August 2017. Many other friends and colleagues helped make this work possible, notably N.R. Visalatchy, S.S. Rangacharyulu, Milan Kumar Chauley, M. Pandu Ranga Rao, Surendra Kumar, and Y. Gangadhar. To all these individuals he would like to express his sincere appreciation.

INTRODUCTION

PREVIOUS PAGES Hanamkonda, Padmakshi Temple, priest attending the goddess decorated with garlands, with painted Jain images cut into the rock to the side

BELOW Warangal, view from Ekashila Hill across the lake to the ruined granary

GEOGRAPHY AND PREHISTORY OF TELANGANA

Telangana may be India's 29th and newest state (2014), but the region has a distinctive identity going back at least to the beginning of the 2nd millennium BCE, and arguably, even to prehistoric times. In terms of physical geography, Telangana may be defined as the northeastern part of the Deccan plateau, an elevated semi-arid tableland bounded north and south by the Godavari and Krishna rivers. On the east, it is fringed by the densely forested hills that separate it from coastal Andhra, and to the west it is demarcated by the zone where Telangana's sandy red soils yield to the black cotton soils of northern Karnataka and Maharashtra. Like much of the rest of the Deccan, Telangana saw a succession of prehistoric and early cultures, beginning with the Southern Neolithic (ca 2,500 to 800 BCE) and the Megalithic (also called Pandukal Complex; ca 800 BCE to 2nd or 3rd century CE). By the beginning of the Common Era, the Megalithic was giving way to the Early Historic Period throughout

most of the region. This was characterized by the rise of larger towns and an expansion of trade, the appearance of coinage and writing, widespread cultural contacts with northern India, and the emergence of state society as represented by the Satavahana kingdom (mid-1st century BCE), arising in the Telangana region and then spreading into the northwestern Deccan.

The emergence of Telangana as a more distinct cultural zone was closely tied to two interlinked developments: the construction of irrigation tanks, known locally as *cheruvus*, which made wet-rice cultivation possible throughout much of this semi-arid region, and the rise and expansion of the Kakatiya state in the second half of the 12th century. Ruling from their capital in the northeastern part of Telangana – first Hanamkonda, and later Warangal – the Kakatiyas quickly expanded their rule over most of the three regions where Telugu is spoken today: Telangana, coastal Andhra, and Rayalaseema in southwestern Andhra.

THE KAKATIYAS AND THEIR SUCCESSORS

Like their contemporaries in other parts of the Deccan – the Yadavas of Devagiri (later renamed Daulatabad) in Maharashtra to the northwest, and the Hoysalas of Dvarasamudra (Halebid) in Karnataka to the southwest – the **Kakatiyas** began their political career as minor feudatories of the Chalukyas of Kalyana (997-1200), an imperial dynasty based in northern Karnataka. In fact, the Kakatiyas' lineage can be traced back even farther, to the middle of the 10th century, when they were local chiefs serving under the Rashtrakutas, but it was only in the early 12th century, under **Prola II** (r. 1116-57), that they fully emerge into the light of history. Prola was responsible for subjugating a number of other local chiefs in Telangana, and his son **Rudradeva** (r. 1157-95) continued his father's expansion of territory, making major inroads into coastal Andhra, and taking advantage of Kalachuri Bijjala's usurpation of the Chalukya throne to declare his own independence in 1163. This moment was marked by Rudradeva's establishment of the so-called Thousand-Pillared Temple in his capital city of Hanamkonda, and his setting up in its courtyard of a foundation inscription. This describes his victories, but conspicuously omits any reference to a Chalukya overlord (see Appendix No. 4). The Thousand-Pillared Temple is the first great monument of Kakatiya architecture. Although Hanamkonda was the first Kakatiya capital, it was quickly superseded by Warangal, the new, planned city which Rudradeva is credited with having founded to the southeast of Hanamkonda.

Rudradeva died without a male heir and was succeeded by his younger brother **Mahadeva** (r. 1195-98), who ruled only a brief three years. In his last year, Mahadeva led a campaign against the neighboring Yadava kingdom, but perished in battle. The victorious Yadava ruler Jaitrapala showed his magnanimity by rescuing Mahadeva's young son, **Ganapatideva** (r. 1199-1262), and placing him on the throne of the Kakatiya kingdom. Ganapati turned his attention to further expansion of his territory all the way to the Bay of Bengal coast, from Nellore in the south to Bokkera in Kalinga (Odisha) in the north. Although the reign began with the fate of the Kakatiyas hanging in the balance, it closed with the kingdom at its apogee, both politically and culturally. In all likelihood, it was during Ganapati's reign that Warangal's inner stone wall was constructed, and that the temple of Svayambhu Shiva, the Kakatiyas' state deity, was given its full-fledged form. Local feudatory rulers and members of the various chiefly families around Telangana likewise took up building projects and contributed to the flourishing state of temple architecture during the period of Ganapati's long reign.

OPPOSITE
Inscription of Rudradeva recording the foundation of the temple at Hanamkonda in 1163, and describing his victories

Like Rudradeva, Ganapati, too, produced no male heir, but invited his daughter **Rudramadevi** (r. 1262-89) to rule as co-regent during the last years of his reign. Upon his death she assumed the throne, and led the Kakatiya armies against incursions of the Pandyas from the south, the Gangas from Odisha to the northeast, and the Yadavas to the west. Toward the end of her reign, the Kayastha chief Ambadeva made a bid for independence by conquering a number of feudatories who had been subordinate to the Kakatiyas, depriving the kingdom of most of its territories south of the Krishna river. Some historians have suggested that it was Rudramadevi's departure from more typical gender roles that led to such widespread opposition to this "female king"; it certainly seems significant that she was frequently referred to in contemporary inscriptions with the masculine form of her name -- Rudradeva -- and was accorded the masculine title "Maharaja". An inscription from Chandupatla in Nalgonda District suggests that she may have died on the battlefield at the age of nearly 80 years.

Rudramadevi's grandson **Prataparudra** (r. 1289-1323) was the last ruler of the Kakatiya kingdom. He began his reign by campaigning against the rebel Ambadeva, and within several years had succeeded in vanquishing the upstart. But before long Prataparudra faced a devastating series of military campaigns from the north, launched by the Delhi Sultanate. These campaigns were initiated by the Sultan **Ala al-Din Khalaji** (r. 1296-1316), proceeding via Bengal in 1302-03. Although this campaign was unsuccessful, he sent his subordinate Malik Kafur six years later, this time via the Yadava kingdom (1309). After a siege of several

Warangal, stone wall and one of the gateways of the fort built by the Kakatiya king Ganapatideva

months, Prataparudra surrendered and became a tributary of the Delhi sultan (1310). But by1318, Prataparudra was in arrears on his tribute payments, and so two more campaigns were launched, the final one by Ulugh Khan (1321-22), who would soon occupy the throne of Delhi as **Muhammad bin Tughluq** (r. 1321-51). Ulugh Khan succeeded in capturing Prataparudra, who appears to have died while being taken as a captive to Delhi.

From 1323 until 1331, Warangal was named as Sultanpur and remained firmly under the control of Delhi. The city's Tughluq rulers patronized several building projects that changed the city's urban fabric; most notably, dismantling the Svayambhu Shiva temple and building a massive congregational mosque on its site, and constructing a monumental stone audience hall, known today as the Khush Mahal, just to the west of the Svayambhu Shiva site. Significantly, some members of

the local elite who had previously served the Kakatiyas were recruited to help administer the city. Nagaya Ganna, for example, who had been the commander of the Warangal fort under Prataparudra, converted to Islam, and with the new name of Malik Maqbul became governor of Sultanpur after Ulugh Khan. Ganna/Maqbul is emblematic of the complex cultural negotiations and interactions that characterized Telangana during this period. Thus, before the Delhi Sultanate's conquests, he had patronized the poet Marana, commissioning him to produce a Telugu translation of the Sanskrit *Markandeya Puranam*, while after he had moved to Delhi he was active in the Hindavi literary circle in which Mawlana Daud wrote his influential Sufi romance *Chandayan*. His tomb may still be seen today in Delhi, in the funerary complex of Nizam al-Din Auliya.

It was not long until a number of local Telugu chiefs joined forces to end Delhi's occupation of the old Kakatiya capital. With Delhi's

Warangal, Khush Mahal, entrance to the audience hall erected during the Tughluq occupation of the city

influence out of the way, a number of these chiefly families held sway over Warangal and the broader Telangana region. The Musunuri chief **Kapaya Nayaka** (r. 1336-68) displaced Malik Maqbul from Warangal in 1336 and ruled the city until about 1368, invoking the authority of the bygone Kakatiya dynasty. Kapaya Nayaka soon came into conflict with the the **Bahmani Sultanate**, which had been founded in 1347 by a faction of commanders and officers who had formerly served Delhi. When Kapaya Nayaka was killed in battle, control of Telangana passed to **Anapota Nayaka** (r. 1368-84) of the Recherla Nayaka family. By 1435, the Bahmani Sultanate had displaced the Recherla Nayakas from northern Telangana and Warangal, pushing them back to their original core territories around Devarakonda and Rachakonda, and leaving Warangal and northeastern Telangana under a Bahmani governor. Except for a brief period between 1460 and 1464 – when the city was captured by an army of the Gajapatis of Kalinga, and then entrusted to the Recherla Nayaka chief Ravu Dharmanayaka – the Bahmanis retained control of Warangal. In 1504, **Shitab Khan** (r. 1504-ca 1516), a Persianized Hindu commander who had earlier been in the service of the Bahmanis, captured Warangal from its Bahmani governor and attempted to revive the Kakatiya imperium.

In about 1512, Shitab Khan was ousted from Warangal by the Bahmani commander **Sultan Quli Qutb al-Mulk** (r. 1518-43). Sultan Quli became the founder of the Qutb Shahi kingdom of Golconda, one of the three most important successor states to emerge from the ashes of the Bahmani Sultanate when it finally collapsed in the decades after 1500. Warangal continued as a major town during the Qutb Shahi period, and exercised an impact on the design of Hyderabad, the new capital laid out by Sultan Muhammad Quli Qutb Shah in 1591. The Qutb Shahis would rule until 1687, the year of the final conquest of the kingdom by the northern Indian Mughal Emperor Aurangzeb (r. 1658-1707).

Warangal, arched gateway in the western walls of the city, added during the Bahmani period

TEMPLE TYPES AND MODES

During the Kakatiya period, the characteristic form of monumental architecture was the temple (*gudi, devalayam*), the majority of which enshrined stone images of Shiva in his characteristic form as the *linga*. A much smaller number of temples dedicated to various forms of Vishnu were also built, but temple worship in Kakatiya Telangana was primarily a Shaiva undertaking. In the earliest period, before the rise of the Kakatiyas as an independent kingdom, Jainism was an important cultural and religious force in the Deccan, and rock-cut caves and images dedicated to the Tirthankaras and to Jain goddesses are also found in Telangana. It is significant that one of these goddesses, Padmakshi, with her temple inside the fort at Hanamkonda, was by the 16th century retrospectively identified as the tutelary goddess of the Kakatiya dynasty. Shaiva monastic institutions, such as the Golaki Matha, representing a branch of Siddhanta Shaivism, were important throughout the Kakatiya realm, and the royal preceptors of the Kakatiyas were selected from this lineage.

From the perspective of plan and spatial layout, Telangana's temples fall into three main types. Most common is the **single-shrined temple**, at the heart of which is a cubical sanctuary occupied by an image of the consecrated deity. The doorway providing the entrance to

Palampet, single-shrined Gaurisha Temple, an example of the Bhumija mode

the sanctuary defines the direction toward which the temple as a whole is oriented. The doorway is generally preceded by a small entrance vestibule, which is in turn most frequently coordinated with a larger pillared hall, or *mandapa*. Nearly as common in the Telangana region is the **triple-shrined temple**, in which three separate shrine units are attached to three sides of the *mandapa*, leaving the fourth side for an entrance porch. This triple-shrined plan is described in contemporary inscriptions as *trikuta*, "three-peaked", with reference to the three towers marking the shrines and symbolically equating each one with the cosmic mountain at the centre of the universe.

The third type of temple layout is a special variant of the single-shrined type in which all four sides of the sanctuary are pierced by doorways. It is known in architectural treatises as **Sarvatobhadra**, literally "auspicious on all sides". This centrally planned temple type is associated with the symbolism of imperial dominion, and represents a microcosm of the larger universe; not surprisingly, the only place the type is attested in Kakatiya Telangana is at the midpoint of the capital city of Warangal, in the temple that housed the Kakatiyas' state deity, Svayambhu Shiva. The *linga* enshrined in this temple was four-faced, allowing Shiva to direct his beneficent gaze out into each of the four directions over which the god ruled. Each doorway was preceded by a *mandapa*, and beyond that by a smaller *mandapa* housing an image of Shiva's bull Nandi. There is additionally a post-Kakatiya period, Sarvatobhadra temple at Nainpak, not far from Ghanpur, which may be dated to the mid-15th century.

In addition to this classification by plan type, Kakatiya temples can be distinguished by their use of different **architectural modes** – that is, different formal systems for articulating the exterior of the temple. These modes can be compared to the different orders in Classical Greek and Roman architecture – such as Doric, Ionic, Corinthian, Tuscan, and so on – which provided different formal options and proportions for articulating the surfaces of buildings. Two of the modes common in Telangana – Vesara and Bhumija – were both derived from earlier architectural traditions of the Kalyana Chalukyas. Although adapted for construction in stone, both modes evolved from a style of timber construction that was originally used in the context of palatial architecture. It is the treatment of the walls that most readily serves to differentiate the two modes. In both modes, the walls are typically divided by various projections and recesses into a rhythmic series of vertical member. A central buttress projecting out from the middle of each wall of the sanctuary is flanked by a receding pair of counter-buttresses, and then a pair of corner elements, which establish the base-line of the wall from which the other members project. In the **Vesara** mode, each of these projections is demarcated by a pair of slender, attenuated pilasters topped by a series of capitals that support the projecting eaves of the building. In the **Bhumija** mode, in contrast, each vertical member is articulated as a single, broad pilaster, creating a very different effect that accentuates the horizontal moldings of the pilasters. In both Vesara and Bhumija, the recesses between the pilasters are often decorated with shallow pillars carrying miniature temple towers. Both modes articulate the tower over the sanctuary in the form of a condensed series of palace storeys, with small shrine-like forms demarcating the perimeter of each level. Very few Kakatiya temples have well-preserved towers; that of the Ramappa temple at Palampet and those of the small subsidiary shrines at Ghanpur being among the clearest and most complete examples. This poor preservation of the towers appears connected to the choice of material. Towers were often constructed not from stone but more often from brick, which when a temple became abandoned could be more easily dilapidated, and then robbed for ready-made building materials.

See photograph on page 22

The third major mode, termed **Phamsana**, is visually quite distinct, and harks back to the masonry forms of the dolmens and cists made by the peoples of the Megalithic era. Unlike either Vesara or Bhumija, the walls of Phamsana-mode sanctuaries lack both vertical pilasters and vertical articulation by means of projections and recesses (although many have extremely shallow and broad buttresses projecting from the planes of the corners); instead they present a continuous expanse of smoothly dressed stone slabs. Above the walls, the superstructure takes the form of a pyramidal sequence of horizontal layers, each articulated by means of a simple cornice molding separated from the previous layer by a deep shadowy recess. The body of the superstructure is surmounted by a square-to-dome roof.

Just as the Classical orders bore specific associations that made them more appropriate in some contexts than in others – the masculine strength of the Doric, for example, being deemed appropriate for temples of masculine deities, and the delicate

OPPOSITE
Palampet, Ramappa Temple main shrine, principal example of the Vesara mode in Kakatiya architecture

softness of the Corinthian for those of goddesses and nymphs – so too with the modes in Kakatiya architecture, although the associated meanings were of course different. The Vesara and Bhumija modes both utilized forms that had been derived from palatial architecture and thus were most often used for temples housing public cults that were inclusive in nature and served to integrate various segments of society. This is seen most clearly in a common type of triple-shrined temple dedicated to the cult of the Tripurushas; that is, the three gods Shiva, Vishnu, and Surya. These temples are in all cases oriented with their entrance porches to the south, and their deities are always in the same fixed location with respect to each other: Shiva on the west, Vishnu on the north, and Surya on the east. These temples would have helped integrate the worship of the two main sectarian deities Shiva and Vishnu. Moreover, all documented examples have additional architectural features that bespeak the presence of large groups of worshippers: monumental detached secondary pillared halls, known as *asthana-mandapas* (literally "court pavilion"), and broad raised platforms providing for circumambulation of numerous people around the exterior of the temple proper.

In contrast, the Phamsana mode appears to have been favoured for more exclusive, family-focused memorial shrines, presumably because of its formal resonances with dolmens from the earlier Megalithic culture. These Phamsana-mode temples usually enshrine Shiva *lingas* named after the donor, or, in the case of triple-shrines, after a triad of members of the donor's family. Thus, for example, the triple-shrined temple on the west end of the earthen wall, or *bund*, that contains the great *cheruvu* at Palampet was established by the general Recherla Rudra, with *lingas* named Kateshvara (Lord of Kataya), Kameshvara (Lord of Kamambika), and Rudreshvara (Lord of Rudra), in honour of his father Kataya, his mother Kamambika, and himself (Appendix No. 5). This naming convention, quite common throughout the Deccan, served to "mark" the *linga* so as to divert at least part of the merit accruing from its worship to its "owner" rather than to the individual performing the act. The establishment of three such *lingas* within a single, triple-shrined temple would additionally have served as monumental testimony to the solidarity of the family unit.

In addition to the temple proper consisting of its shrine(s) and main *mandapa*, a number of ancillary structures are frequently met with,

Palampet, Golla Gudi, ruined example of a triple-shrined temple in Phamsana mode

especially in larger temples. The sacred precinct is often demarcated from its surroundings by a stone enclosure wall with an upper walkway protected by spade-shaped merlons. Shiva temples are sometimes provided with a small pavilion housing the image of Shiva's bull-vehicle Nandi. This is invariably positioned on axis with the main doorway of the temple proper and consists of a single open-pillared bay, generally with either a single doorway toward the main shrine, or a pair of doorways, one toward the outside and the other toward the shrine. In the more monumental, inclusive temples in Vesara or Bhumija mode, both triple-shrined and single-shrined, an expansive ***asthana-mandapa*** is provided, located inevitably to the south of the temple proper. As represented at Hanamkonda, Manthani, Palampet, and Ghanpur, these halls are square in plan but with projecting extensions in the middle of each side, and with further, smaller projections from the faces of these. The forms of these buildings reflect the inventiveness of the Kakatiya architects and their engagement with complex problems of architectural design. In ritual terms, it is not at all clear what were the intended functions of these *asthana-mandapas*. Today they are popularly referred to as a *kalyana-mandapa*; that is, a hall where the annual festival of the marriage

of the god and goddess is celebrated. But the *kalyana-mandapa* as a type is more associated with the Vijayanagara and even later periods, and there is no real evidence to suggest that the Kakatiya period *asthana-mandapas* ever served such a purpose. What is useful to note is that *asthana-mandapas* are in all documented cases located to the south of the temple to which they are subordinated, and that they appear to have functioned as gateway pavilions, where worshippers might meet and interact before entering the temple proper. With their projecting rhythms and complex juxtaposition of colonnades of varying heights, these *asthana-mandapas* are among the most innovative architectural achievements of the designers and builders who served the Kakatiyas and their subordinates.

Perhaps the most emblematic architectural form of the Kakatiyas is the ritual gateway known as a ***torana***. These somewhat distant and austere descendants of the better-known *toranas* of ancient Buddhist sites such as Sanchi and Bharhut in central India feature prominently in the Svayambhu Shiva temple at the centre of Warangal. There they serve not as actual physical entrances to the temple compound, but rather as symbolic markers of the four quarters of the cosmos over which the Kakatiyas aspired to rule. Ainavolu, just south of Warangal, is another site where *toranas* of this form were used. It appears likely that they were copied from Warangal's *toranas* under the patronage of the Recherla chief Anapota Nayaka in about 1369. In any case, the form of the Warangal *toranas* has been endlessly repeated in full-scale replicas and in contemporary advertising as symbolic expressions of Telugu identity. It also forms part of the seal of Telangana State.

OPPOSITE
Warangal, one of the four monumental *toranas* defining the compound of the Svayambhu Shiva temple, which was later demolished

PATTERNS OF TEMPLE PATRONAGE

Turning now to consider the foundation and construction of new temples, two important patterns of patronage should be noted. The first is that there is very little evidence of direct **royal sponsorship** by members of the Kakatiya family. The only surviving major temple complex definitively know to have been founded by a ruling Kakatiya king is the Thousand-Pillared Temple at Hanamkonda, a product of Rudradeva's patronage. The Svayambhu Shiva temple at Warangal must also have been a royal foundation, given that it was the Kakatiyas' state deity, but little of this survives. There is also epigraphic evidence attesting that Ganapatideva founded at least one important temple at the capital, known as Sahasralinga Ganapatishvara, a thousand-shafted *linga* founded in Ganapati's name. This temple continued to receive gifts even into Prataparudra's time, and these were made in the presence of the Kakatiya royal preceptor, attesting to the temple's continuing importance. But the vast majority of so-called Kakatiya temples were in fact not established by members of the Kakatiya family, but rather by their **feudatories, subordinates, and officers**. In fact, some of the most important patrons of temple construction in this period were members of the Recherla family, one of whom, Recherla Rudra, belonging to the Yelkurti branch of the family, was responsible for the justly famous temples at Palampet. Members of the other, Pillalamarri branch of the Recherla family financed the construction of temples at Pillalamarri and Nagulapadu in Nalgonda District (not included in this guidebook).

The other pattern of patronage to note here has to do with chronology. The heyday of temple construction in the Kakatiya realm was during the reigns of Rudradeva and Ganapatideva; that is, from about the middle of the 12th century through the middle of the 13th century. During that period, there was a veritable profusion of new foundations, in many cases linked with construction of substantial *cheruvus*. There is thus a clear connection between temple foundations and economic development, as previously un-irrigated portions of Telangana were being brought under intensive regimes of wet-rice agriculture. After the mid-13th century, however, the construction of new temples slows down and eventually ceases altogether by about 1276, the year of the last documented consecration of a new temple in Kakatiya Telangana, the Gundeshvara temple at Bhutpur in Mahboobnagar District (not described here). This decline in patronage must have been directly linked to the fact that the region was already as fully developed as was sustainable in that era. The plain and unrefined forms of the Bhutpur temple suggest the impact that lack of employment must have had on the guilds of architects and sculptors whose ancestors had produced such masterpieces as the Ramappa temple at Palampet. Telangana's tradition of temple architecture was thus practically defunct long before the conquests of the region by the Delhi Sultanate.

ENGINEERING AND CONSERVATION

Many temples of Kakatiya Telangana, including some of those described in this guidebook, are today in a poor state of preservation, with their columns out of plumb, beams broken, and some bays even collapsed. While some of this damage may be from local seismic activity induced by nearby reservoirs, much more is due to the nature of the foundations typically used in Kakatiya temple architecture. Exemplary research by Professor M. Pandu Ranga Rao and his colleagues at the Regional Engineering College at Warangal has demonstrated that the builders in this tradition employed the so-called **sand-box method** for constructing foundations. According to this practice, a pit is dug in the ground and a stone retaining wall is constructed around the edges of the pit. The enclosed space is then filled with sand and compacted, and the stone construction proceeds upward on the base of packed sand. As long as the sand remains intact, this provides for a firm and stable foundation, but should there be any underground water flow, the sand will gradually percolate out, leaving a cavity into which elements of the temple structure can sink. This process accounts for the sanctuary walls sinking into the platform at the Kota Gudi at Ghanpur, and for the breaking and upheaval of the floor beams surrounding the circular, raised podium in the middle of the floor of the main hall, or *ranga-mandapa*, of the Ramappa temple at Palampet. Pandu Ranga Rao has in recent years worked in collaboration with the Archaeological Survey of India to formulate and implement the engineering aspect of conservation plans for several of the monuments covered in this book. At the Thousand-Pillared Temple, the *asthana-mandapa* has had its unusually long stone beams repaired and reinforced, and at this time of writing is still underway. It is hoped that the Ramappa temple's *asthana-mandapa* will soon be the next major monument to be restored.

See photograph on pages 52-53

HANAMKONDA

PREVIOUS PAGES Hanamkonda, Thousand-Pillared Temple, Nandi and *asthana-mandapa* (photograph by Deen Dayal, 1888: Courtesy The Alkazi Collection of Photography)

HANAMKONDA FORT

The Kakatiyas had their first capital at Hanamkonda (variants Hanumakonda, Anumakonda), where they took advantage of a flat site naturally protected by boulder-strewn outcroppings on three sides, called Padmakshi Gutta (on the west), Gaggaleya Gutta (on the north), and Siddha Gutta (to the east). These natural fortifications were augmented by constructing earthen or stone enclosure walls at ground level so as to close off the spaces between adjacent hills, and filling in gaps between boulders along the ridge of each hill. Most of these man-made additions have disappeared, but small portions of them survive intact here and there, including traces of an earthen wall that would have protected the southern side of the fort where there is no outcropping. The level space thus enclosed amounted to less than 25 hectares, so this was probably the elite zone of the city, and the bulk of the population lived outside the fort proper.

See photograph on page 1

A large *cheruvu*, today known as **Bhadrakali lake**, was eventually constructed to the east of Siddha Gutta, and its impounded waters would have provided an additional obstacle for enemies attacking from the southern side of the fort. This work was undertaken by Betana Pergade, a minister of Prola II, at a date no later than 1117. Contemporary inscriptions mention canals and irrigated fields below the earthen wall, or *bund*, of the tank where wet crops such as rice were cultivated. This agricultural zone would have been primarily located outside the walls on the northeastern side of the city. The majority of the non-elite population would have resided outside the fort in the zone immediately north of Gaggaleya Gutta and Padmakshi Gutta, an area that continues to be heavily populated today. In this neighborhood, small shrines and sculptures dating back to the Kakatiya period can be found in practically every lane. Until the early 1980s, the area inside Hanamkonda Fort was largely empty of constructions other than temples and small tanks, but it has since been developed and is now home to several educational institutions, businesses, and residential neighborhoods.

A single gateway doorframe still stands in place in the middle of the modern roadway at a point that must have been the main **northern entrance** to Hanamkonda Fort. That there was a fortification wall here is attested by the two parallel rows of footing sockets that were carved into the sheetrock rising up steeply just east of the doorway. These would have served to anchor wall slabs that have since disappeared. On the southeastern side of the fort, two more similar doorframes stand in between the southeastern hill and the nearby earthen wall to the west; together with the partial remains of a third doorframe, these structures suggest a large **bent-axis gateway** with an imposing gatehouse of a form seen in the gateways of the stone walls of Warangal Fort. Given the poor state of its preservation, it is not clear whether this gateway was a creative innovation where the bent-axis plan was first worked out, or what is perhaps more likely, a later modification of a single-door gateway inspired by Warangal's gateways.

Doorframe of the gateway on the southeastern side of Hanamkonda Fort

Rock-cut Jain images on Gaggaleya Gutta

JAIN VESTIGES ON GAGGALEYA GUTTA

Before entering Hanamkonda Fort itself, the intrepid visitor may wish to climb up the outer, northern side of Gaggaleya Gutta, following a rough path that takes off up the hill from the left side of the road a short distance before the fort's entrance. The reward is a view of a group of **Jain sculptures**, carved into the cliff face above, which constitute some of the earliest monumental vestiges at the site. Ascending this path, one soon arrives at a panel carved into the rock face featuring seven standing Jain Tirthankaras, including two with cobra hoods (Neminatha and Parshvanatha) and five others with no distinguishing iconographic attributes. This is one of the few groups of Jain images at Hanamkonda that has not been painted over. They most likely date to the Rashtrakuta period, about the middle of the 10th century. Further to the east is a large Shantinatha image, now painted, and recognizable by the tiny deer emblem carved at the figure's feet. A short distance still further to the east is a small, unfinished cave excavation, divided into three bays by two pillars and side pilasters. One can see here the technique that was used for excavating – the outlines were chiselled away, leaving a projecting rectangular mass of stone, which was then detached intact by a few well-placed chisel blows. A short distance further beyond this to the east is a finished (unpainted) panel of a standing Parshvanatha and, to its side on the right, an unfinished carving of a seated figure, probably a Tirthankara.

Backtracking and going a short distance to the west of the path the visitor will come upon the best preserved segment of the man-made **fortification wall** that was added to supplement the boulders of the hill itself. Approaching from the direction of the carved Jain images, one will see the outside face of this wall, which has been executed from carefully cut ashlar masonry with long stretchers and intermittent headers to tie together the outer and inner faces of the wall. Going around through several narrow openings between adjacent boulders, one can approach the rear side of this wall, which is unusual and noteworthy for its projecting header ends providing a handhold for defenders to climb up to the rampart at the top. This rampart is made from overhanging cantilevered slabs projecting back toward the inner side of the wall at the top, and it features a number of steps at places where the wall follows the changing elevation of the fort. On the outside face, there are remnants of a parapet atop the battlement.

PADMAKSHI AND SIDDHESHVARA TEMPLES

Entering Hanamkonda Fort from the north, the visitor will pass through the remnants of the above-mentioned stone gateway. After a short distance, one notices to the right the painted yellow tower of the **Padmakshi temple** rising up from the rocky crags of the outcropping. A flight of steps leads from the road up to the temple, where a simple ritual doorway opens into an exterior courtyard before the temple proper. The temple consists of an enclosed *mandapa* and a grotto-like sanctuary. Unlike most temples, this one "borrows" for its walls the irregular forms of several boulders, atop which rises the attenuated sanctuary tower.

In the exterior courtyard, there is a prominent stone stele carved with an inscription dated to 1117, during the reign of Kakatiya Prola II. It records that Mailama, the wife of Prola's minister Betana Pergade, established on the top of the hill a Jain temple, the Kadalalaya Basadi, and donated lands for its support and daily worship. It has been suggested that "Kadalalaya" is a Kannada name for the Jain goddess Padmavati, the female protective deity of the 23rd Tirthankara, Parshvanatha. If so that would suggest that the goddess today worshipped as the Shaivite goddess Padmakshi was originally the Jain goddess Padmavati, and that as Jainism was eclipsed by the rise of Shaivism, the goddess's identity was reinterpreted accordingly. (This

వరంగల్.

developmental pattern was being recognized by local brahmin scholars already by the early nineteenth century; see Appendix No. 1.) The image of Padmakshi is of high relief, carved out of the face of the boulder that defines the back wall of the temple. To her proper right are carved relief images of Parshvanatha and Dharanendra, further supporting the interpretation that Padmakshi originated as a Jain goddess. Very little of the original sculpture can be seen due to the fact that Padmakshi has been dressed in a rich silk sari, provided with silver repoussé armour for her arms, and bedecked with jewels, ornaments, and flowers. Her face is covered with turmeric or sandalwood paste.

See photograph on pages 12-13

Several other **Jain images** can be seen within the temple as well as numerous Jain sculptures adorning the face of the adjacent cliff and boulders. Particularly noteworthy is an unusual three-storeyed shrine model kept in the sanctuary, carved with images of the 24 Tirthankaras, three on each of the four sides of the lower level, two on each side of the middle level, and one on each side of the top cupola. Outside, beyond the west side of the temple, there is an opening in the cliff face, leading to an interconnected network of natural caves under the boulders, which may have been used for shelter by Jain mendicants in the site's earliest period. To the right of this entrance, the cliff face has been carved with several relief sculptures depicting Jain deities. These include a large standing Parshvanatha, and, to the left of that, a smaller tableau with a Parshvanatha seated on a lion throne, flanked by male fly-whisk bearers. To the left and slightly below this image a male

OPPOSITE Stepped path leading up to Padmakshi Temple

LEFT Painted, rock-cut images of Parshvanatha and donor figures in the Padmakshi Temple

the triple-shrined, main temple. This structure has for many years been in an advanced state of dilapidation, but it has always been admired for its profusion of columns, both standing and collapsed (actually numbering 120, counting pilasters as well as free-standing columns). The *mandapa* is now being altogether rebuilt, with the work estimated to be completed by 2020.

In addition to its innovative design and exceptional quality, the Thousand-Pillared Temple is of outstanding historical significance, since its foundation represented the Kakatiyas' first public statement of independence from their erstwhile overlords, the Kalyana Chalukyas. It is the undeniable masterpiece of 12th-century Kakatiya architecture. It also happens to be the only intact building that was the result of a direct royal foundation; the vast majority of surviving Kakatiya foundations resulted from the patronage of feudatory chiefs or military officers of the Kakatiyas.

The **compound** of the Thousand-Pillared Temple is accessed through a wide corridor planted with gardens running off of the south side of the main Hyderabad-Warangal road, at a point about 750 metres east of Hanumakonda Chaurashtha, the city's main intersection. Entering the gate, the visitor will proceed south past a water tank on the left; the temple will be ahead and to the right. The temple consists of three main units, all connected by a common raised platform: to the north, a triple-shrined temple proper, consisting of three sanctuary-and-vestibule units attached to three sides of a nine-bayed *ranga-mandapa*, with a two-bayed porch on the fourth side orienting the complex to the south. South of that are the remnants of a small Nandi pavilion, with its larger than life-sized bull, still beautifully preserved. Combining as it does a generally convincing life-like naturalism with a tendency toward abstraction, this sculpture is one of the masterpieces of Kakatiya art. As in much other Kakatiya sculpture, the mass of the body has been reduced to a series of interlocking, curving planes that nonetheless are effective in conveying a sense of organic, living presence. Still further to the south is a monumental and innovative *asthana-mandapa*, its overall plan almost exactly the same size as that of the temple proper. The foundation inscription, incised into an imposing stone stele standing just inside the eastern entrance to the compound, records that the temple was dedicated to the cult of the Tripurushas: Shiva as "Rudreshvara", on the west and oriented east; Vishnu as "Vasudevara", on the north,

See photograph on page 16

Thousand-Pillared Temple, Nandi

oriented south; and the sun god Surya as "Suryadevara" on the east, oriented west (see Appendix No. 4). In the western shrine, the *linga* of Rudreshvara is still present and is attended by a temple priest. The images of Vishnu and Surya that once occupied the north and east shrines are no longer preserved.

The Thousand-Pillared Temple stands on a **broad terrace** that provides an elevated, open path for circumambulation. Access to the terrace is via two paired flights of steps, one pair on either side of the Nandi pavilion, one before it and one behind it. Circumambulating at this level provides the visitor with the best way of appreciating the intricate forms of the temple proper. The exterior of each of the **three shrine units** of the temple is articulated in the Bhumija mode, and is divided into seven projecting divisions shaped like broad column shafts, and separated by narrow recesses, each ornamented with a tower-on-pilaster motif. The vertical lines of the pillar shafts and pilaster motifs are counterbalanced by the prominence of the plinth and frieze upon which the pilaster shafts sit, and of the continuous entablature they carry, thus providing a strong horizontal accent. Although no longer preserved, each shrine unit would have carried a Bhumija superstructure, consisting of miniature temple

Thousand-Pillared Temple

ABOVE View from the southeast

FOLLOWING PAGE LEFT External wall niche of the eastern sanctuary

FOLLOWING PAGE RIGHT Interior of the *ranga-mandapa*

towers carried on columns arrayed above each pilaster of the wall, and rising up through a series of levels. In the middle of each wall of the three shrines, a miniature shrine niche projects from the central buttress, taking the form of a small three-towered temple. Each niche would originally have contained a sculpture of some form of the deity enshrined within, but these have disappeared. Locations where sculptures may be still seen are against the central projection of the vestibule, and against the corner shafts of each shrine. In each case, these sculptures portray various forms of the deity housed within the shrine. The dancing Ganesha on the south side of the vestibule of the Rudreshvara shrine is especially memorable.

Continuing around clockwise, the visitor will notice a water spout exiting the middle of the north wall of the Rudreshvara shrine at the level of the uppermost block of the plinth, which corresponds to the interior floor level. The purpose of this spout is to capture and channel the holy water from bathing the deity inside so it can be distributed to worshippers in the course of their devotions. The water issues out from inside the sanctuary and down a small hollow column, into the masonry of the basement, whence it flows out through a second spout at the level of the plinth and into a pot where it is collected. In the case of the other two shrines, the spout issues on the east side of the Vasudevara shrine and the north side of the Surya shrine. Turning left and walking north parallel to the western wall of the Vasudevara shrine, the visitor will notice a subtle difference in the treatment of the mouldings at the bottom of the wall (*vedika*); here in this shrine alone they are treated as a second, reduplicated set of plinth mouldings.

Entering the porch of the Thousand-Pillared Temple, the

Thousand-Pillared Temple

ABOVE Ceiling in the *ranga-mandapa*

OPPOSITE Column in the *ranga-mandapa*

visitor will ascend a short flight of steps that leads to the interior of the ***ranga-mandapa***. Whereas the exterior of the temple is constructed from gray granite, the principal structural elements of the hall interior are made of fine-grained and highly polished black dolerite. This stone has an extremely high compressive strength, and is thus perfectly suited for such use. The four central columns take an ornate form with their shafts each articulated into two square-sectioned blocks separated by a recessed circular section carved with alternating raised octagonal and circular bands of ornate jewels. The rest of the shaft, and the sequence of three capitals that it carries above, are equally ornately carved and polished to a high metallic sheen. Above, the beams of the central bay and the triangular slabs of the three-tiered lantern ceiling they support are likewise of dolerite. Both the inner and outer faces of the ceiling beams are carved in a crisp but restrained manner, with jewelled friezes on outer and inner sides, and a single projecting lotus rosette in the middle of the underside. Each triangular slab is carved with a monster mask, or *kirtimukha*, while the topmost square slab is carved with an image of Shiva dancing, surrounded by the gods of the eight directions. The remaining bays of the *ranga-mandapa* and of the porch are likewise supported by triangular corner slabs, but only in two tiers. These are of granite and feature simpler and more geometric designs.

An inscription carved into the surface of the northeastern column records a visit to the temple by one Vibhuti Gauraya, a native of Machirajupalli in Warangal, who came seeking refuge. It further records that he was a servant in the household of the great Shaiva teacher Mallikarjuna Panditaradhya (ca 1100-85), who resided on the peak of the sacred mountain at Srisailam, a holy spot on the Krishna river in Rayalseema. This would put Gauraya's visit in the 20- or 25-year period following the establishment of the temple. Interestingly, Vibhuti Gauraya also recorded his visits to at least eight other temples in Telangana and Rayalaseema, including those at Palampet and Ghanpur, using almost identical wording. At Palampet, he inscribed the graffiti in Telugu and in Sanskrit in both Nandi-Nagari and Grantha script.

The richness of ornately carved dolerite continues in the carving at the entrances to the vestibules of the **sanctuaries** within the Thousand-Pillared Temple. This consists of a pair of trimly proportioned two-block columns flanked by carved stone screens, and carrying an ornate frieze carved with aquatic monsters, or *makaras*, at each end

Thousand-Pillared Temple, doorway leading to the northern (Vasudevara) shrine

and undulating lotus scrolls in between. In the middle of each frieze is a dancing image of the deity housed in the shrine within. Entering the vestibule through this portal, one sees the doorway of the sanctuary ahead and a small secondary shrine on each of the side walls. Marking the pinnacle of the 12th-century Kakatiya sculptor's art, the sanctuary doorways each consist of five ornately carved bands featuring decorative foliage, lions with composite heads, serpent-kings, musicians, and ornate gems; a figure of Gajalakshmi marks the midpoint of the architrave and there are figures of male guardians and of females at the base of the doorjambs at either side.

The ***asthana-mandapa*** to the south of the Nandi pavilion of the Thousand-Pillared Temple represents the first formulation of an architectural type that would continue to be a hallmark of Kakatiya architecture, at least in foundations by the rulers themselves or their highest-ranking officers in their core territories, as at Manthani,

Palampet, and Ghanpur. Like the temple proper, the *asthana-mandapa* sits on an elevated terrace, but it takes a different form, with a central square with broad projections in the middle of each side, and a narrower set of projections from those projections. The *asthana-mandapa* is supported on this platform and follows its layout. Thus, it takes the form of a square pillared hall enclosed by solid walls but pierced by a doorway in the middle of each side; and has a two-tier projection on each side, those on the north and the south taking the form of entrance porches, and those on the east and west sides of balconies, all defined by half-walls with seat-slabs and back-rest slabs. The interior of the *asthana-mandapa* is divided into 25 irregular bays by groups of four columns beyond

Thousand-Pillared Temple, *asthana-mandapa* under restoration in 2018; see also photograph on pages 32-33

the corners of the raised, circular stone marking the hall's central bay. From the exterior, what is most striking about the design of this singular building is the rhythmic alternation between the shorter and squatter columns of the porches and balconies, and the full height but slender columns standing five at each corner of the plan.

Located on the southern side of the Thousand-Pillared Temple complex, and in alignment with the temple's southward facing porch, the monumental *asthana-mandapa* probably served as the primary entrance to the complex. It must have fulfilled a more specific purpose as well, whether ritual or social.

WARANGAL

Already by Rudradeva's reign, the population of the Kakatiya capital at Hanamkonda must have been outgrowing the capacity of the fort and the zone around the Thousand-Pillared Temple to contain it. A new, planned capital was accordingly laid out some 7 kilometres southeast of the old capital, and by 1195, Rudradeva is described in one inscription as ruling from Orugallu (City of One Stone), as the site was called in Telugu, now generally referred to in its Anglicized pronunciation as Warangal. In Sanskrit, the city was known as Ekashila Nagara, which has the same meaning. Both terms refer to the high rocky outcropping rising up in Warangal's southeast quadrant.

CIRCULAR PLAN, FORTIFICATIONS AND GATEWAYS

See map on inside rear jacket

Whatever the pressures of population may have been at Warangal, another factor was clearly the desire to construct a city that would mirror the form of the larger cosmos and thus serve as a fitting residence for the ruler of a kingdom with imperial ambitions. Accordingly, a **circular plan** was adopted, with intersecting north-south and east-west avenues that created a four-quadrant urban plan. This scheme emphasized the central zone of the city where were located the temple of the Kakatiyas' new tutelary deity, Svayambhu Shiva, and the palace of the king who ruled in his name. This layout was modelled on the structure of traditional Indian cosmograms, which featured a circular continent known as Jambudvipa with mount Meru at its centre (the temple of Svayambhu Shiva and its crowning tower), from which rivers flowed in the four directions (the four main roads leading from the central plaza to the city's cardinal gateways). Beyond the edge of Jambudvipa was a ring-shaped sea (the moat outside of the inner stone wall) and beyond that was a second, ring-shaped continent (the space between the inner moat and the outer mud wall) bounded by yet another ring-shaped ocean (the outer moat of the city).

PREVIOUS PAGES
Warangal Fort, southern gateway

OPPPOSITE
Warangal Fort, stone ramparts and moat

Not only does Warangal present one of the earliest and best-preserved specimens of medieval Indian urban planning, it also preserves important evidence of military architecture. Its massive **outer wall** consists of packed earth, produced while excavating the surrounding moat, and averages about 60 metres wide at its base. In those places where it is not badly eroded, this so-called "mud wall" rises up to a height of about 10 metres. It measures approximately 2.4 kilometres in diameter, enclosing an area of 485 hectares, and access through it is provided by eight passageways, located more or less at the cardinal and intermediate directions. It is not clear how these passageways would originally have been closed off, or how traffic through them might have been regulated; those on the eastern and western sides today take the form of elaborate stone gateways, but these were constructed only in the 15th century. Most of the other gateways in this circuit are overgrown and impassible.

Inside, there is a second, concentric **inner wall** made of earth clad with stone, which measures just over one kilometre in diameter and contains an area of approximately 78 hectares, here referred to as Warangal Fort. The wall is constructed of massive granite slabs encasing an earthen core, averaging about 15 metres in thickness at its base and about 5 to 8 metres in height from ground to battlement walkway. The dressed slabs each measure approximately 1 by 1 by 3 metres, and are tightly fitted together without any mortar. The fabric varies from place to place, but the most common pattern features a regular alternation

Warangal Fort, stepped inner face of the ramparts

of courses, one with the slabs laid as stretchers parallel to the wall's surface, and the next arranged perpendicularly as headers projecting into the earthen core of the wall so as to bond it together more tightly. The wall's inner face is lined with long slabs arranged stepwise and graded at approximately a 30 degree angle, thus providing easy access to the top of the rampart from any point at its base. The battlement walkway averages about 5 to 7 metres in width, and defenders would have been shielded by a low parapet wall topped with diminutive crenellations that seem to have been largely decorative.

Projecting from the outer face of the wall and towering over the surrounding moat are 45 rectangular **bastions** measuring about 12 by 16 metres and spaced at intervals of 60 to 100 metres. Approximately in the middle of each quadrant of the circular wall there is a wider rectangular bastion; close inspection of the masonry joints reveals that these were originally secondary, side gates flanked by paired bastions that have subsequently had their passageways filled in. These may be made out most easily from the outside in the northeast and northwest quadrants. The four main **gateway complexes** likely represent the earliest known examples of the bent-axis gateway type in the Deccan. Each of these is defined by barbican walls that project outward about 55 metres from the main curtain wall and are separated by about 37 metres. Doorways control access to two successive courtyards contained within the gateway; a third doorway controls access to the city within. The doorways were made capacious enough to allow passage to elephants. (Today the elephants have been replaced by municipal buses plying their route through Warangal Fort.)

See photograph on pp. 18-19

SVAYAMBHU SHIVA COMPLEX

The best place for the visitor to begin exploring Warangal is in the zone around the ruins of the temple of Svayambhu Shiva, literally Self-Manifest Shiva, in the middle of the city. According to a story first narrated in the *Prataparudra Charitramu,* this deity manifested himself when king Prola together with his advisors discovered that a *linga* of Shiva had sprouted out of the ground at this very spot, and had the magical power of transforming iron into gold (see Appendix No. 3). Since the *linga* could not be moved to Hanamkonda, the king had a new city constructed with the Self-Manifest Shiva at its centre. Prola's successors devoted themselves to worshipping the feet of Svayambhu Shiva and ruling in the name of the god, and thus was the pre-eminence of the Kakatiya line established.The ruins of Svayambhu Shiva's temple are contained within the central **archaeological zone** of Warangal Fort, which can be entered for a small fee at the ticket booth on its west side.

Upon entering, the visitor is faced with row upon row of stone structural components and sculptural fragments from the ruined temple that have been laid out on the grass, in different groups carefully sorted by color. Toward the right, there are several standing stone columns – the only vertical elements within the enclosure to survive from early times. A short distance ahead and toward the right, one will encounter at ground level the uppermost course of the temple's **stone foundations**. These trace out a cruciform plan consisting of a central square with narrower rectangular projections on each side, and from each of these, a narrow causeway connecting to a smaller square. When intact, this structure would have taken the form of a Sarvatobhadra shrine, housing Svayambhu Shiva's *linga* in a four-door sanctuary at the midpoint of the main square platform. The *linga* would have been of the four-faced (*chatur-mukha*) variety, bearing a high-relief bust of Shiva in anthropomorphic form on each of its four sides, enabling the god to look out in all four directions at the universe over which he rules. This central sanctuary would have been surmounted by a multi-storeyed tower, and surrounded on all four sides by a continuous, open-walled, pillared *mandapa*. Each of the smaller square units at the periphery of the foundations would have carried a pavilion dedicated for a recumbent image of Shiva's bull Nandi, who would have sat devotedly facing in toward his master, one from each of the four sides. The pavilion on the

Svayambhu Shiva Temple

ABOVE View of the reassembled remains

OPPOSITE Basement of one of the four demolished Nandi pavilions

east is sufficiently well-preserved so that one can clearly comprehend its layout.

Although nothing of the Svayambhu Shiva complex is left standing today, there are ample fragmentary remains that confirm the likelihood of this interpretation. Most important is the well-preserved *chatur-mukha linga* carved from black dolerite placed in the courtyard of the Shambhuni Gudi, immediately south of the Svayambhu Shiva enclosure (described below). It is fragmentary, having been severed from the lower portion of its octagonal shaft, and significantly, that missing lower portion of the shaft was found to be lying at a point just 12 metres from the spot it would originally have occupied at the centre of the temple. The fragment has since been moved to the northeastern part of the enclosure, where it has been carefully laid out in the grass together with other fragments from the temple. In similar fashion, there are several oval-shaped bases for Nandi images of the appropriate size for the Nandi pavilions, and at

with a three-by-three grid of small holes meant to contain the ritual deposits inserted to enliven the deity's image.

Before leaving the Svayambhu Shiva enclosure, the visitor should take in the open-air **sculpture garden** that occupies the southwestern portion of the site. These are mostly items that were excavated from

Svayambhu Shiva Temple, fragments displayed in the sculpture garden

the site in the 1920s and 1930s by Ghulam Yazdani, then Director of the Archaeological Department of the Nizam of Hyderabad, although some pieces have also been moved here from other locations. Many of these fragments are stunning and manifest some of the finest quality sculptural carving in all of Kakatiya art. It should be noted, however, that the arrangement of these fragments is fanciful and improvised, rather than presenting reconstructions of any part of the original monument. For example, the carved triangular slabs that are placed vertically over pairs of columns as if they were sculptured pediments were not intended to be displayed that way, but rather lying flat and filling the corners of square ceiling bays. There is also a *linga* installed on an improvised throne-like shrine built out of seat-slabs and back-rest slabs that are properly found only in *mandapas*. (A *linga* when properly consecrated would never be situated in such a location.)

TRACES OF THE JAMI MASJID

Before leaving the central archaeological zone of Warangal Fort, the visitor should take time to seek out the traces of the congregational mosque that was fashioned out of dismantled pieces of the Svayambhu Shiva temple by the army of the Delhi Sultanate. When the conquerors finally reduced Warangal in 1323 and took the king Prataparudra prisoner, they clearly recognized the significance of Svayambhu Shiva to the Kakatiya state. In order to ensure that the deity would not become the focus of attempts to restore the kingdom, the Tughluq army worked systematically to dismantle the temple and to desecrate Svayambhu Shiva's *linga* by breaking it in half. The largest and most ornate pillars from the temple's *mandapas* were carefully salvaged and put aside for reuse, while the remaining structural and decorative elements were broken into fragments and strewn across the site of the erstwhile temple. This rubble was then buried to provide a new, elevated floor level for the plaza lying in between the four *kirti-toranas,* and the portals themselves were carefully preserved to demarcate this central space.

On the western side of the dismantled temple site, the **prayer hall** of a Jami Masjid of vast proportions was constructed, based on the modulus of an octagonal bay inscribed within a square. The width of this modulus was 15 metres, which is 3 metres greater than the prayer hall in the next largest congregational mosque in the Deccan – the Jami Masjid that had been erected just a year earlier at Daulatabad (previously Devagiri). Each of these modular units was defined by eight reused Kakatiya pillars of black dolerite – with all of their figural sculptures carefully chiselled off – with four additional reused pillars of pink granite placed in the corners so as to create a regular, orthogonal grid. How many of these modular units were provided is unclear; a total of either three or five arranged in a roughly north-to-south line would seem likely, but at present the only clear evidence is for a single octagon-in-square bay that would have stood in front of the mosque's central *mihrab*, the arched niche that served as a devotional focus for prayers. All that is left standing of this unit is three of the original dolerite columns, one of the pink granite corner columns, and a much shorter column bearing a second shaft stacked above it. These would have been engaged within the wall to the west that served to mark the *qibla*, giving worshippers the direction of Mecca. Several of the ceiling beams carried by these columns are still intact, shored up by simple square-sectioned piers of

Svayambhu Shiva Temple, remaining pillars of the prayer hall of the Jami Masjid

Svayambhu Shiva Temple, fallen and broken *minbar* pulpit of the Jami Masjid

stone inserted by Yazdani. Above the ceiling beams, the octagonal bay was roofed by a corbelled dome, fragments of which still lie on the ground within the bay. The identification of the structure as a mosque is confirmed by its having been provided with standard mosque features, such as a ***mihrab* niche** and a ***minbar* pulpit**, fragments of which can be identified in the immediate vicinity of the partially preserved bay, as well as by its design, which is closely modelled on that of earlier mosques in Delhi and other Sultanate centres in northern India.

What might account for the ruined condition of this Jami Masjid, which, when intact, would have been one of the most imposing mosques in all of India? One possibility, given the great size of the corbelled domes carried by eight 6-metre long beams atop the columns of the octagonal bay, is that the total load of the dome would have been too great given the lack of strength of the dolerite beams, leading to structural failure and collapse. If that is the case, then this scenario might also account for the fact that there is evidence for only the central *mihrab* bay of the mosque. If indeed the entire edifice had collapsed after constructing this ritually most important part of the mosque, that would plausibly have led to the cessation of any further building activity on the site. A second distinct possibility is that the mosque might, like the temple before it, have been subjected to desecration and dismantlement in the early 1330s, when Warangal was retaken by the local Telugu chief Kapaya Nayaka after he wrested control of the city back from the Tughluqs.

SHAMBHUNI GUDI AND CHAUBARA

Immediately south of the Svayambhu Shiva complex is the Shambhuni Gudi, which appears to have become the primary centre of Shaivite worship after the destruction of the Svayambhu Shiva temple and is still very much alive today. In part this may be due to the fact that, as already mentioned, the top portion of the broken ***chatur-mukha linga*** of Svayambhu Shiva has found its resting place in the courtyard here. In the early 2000s, there were also several large Nandi images located here, of which two or three were good candidates for having originally been installed in the Nandi pavilions of the Svayambhu Shiva.

Shambhuni Gudi, courtyard

RIGHT Broken *chatur-mukha linga* in the courtyard of the Shambhuni Gudi

OPPOSITE Two-storeyed *chaubara*

Just across the street at the back of the Shambhuni Gudi is a single-bayed, **two-storeyed *mandapa*** of Kakatiya date. It has been suggested that this served to ritually demarcate the midpoint of the city of Warangal, and thus would have also commemorated the above-mentioned incident of Svayambhu Shiva's manifestation that led the Kakatiyas to construct the new city. It thus stands as one of the earliest documented instances of a common feature of medieval Deccani cities, referred to as a *chaubara*, located at the central crossing of a city's two main avenues. Other well-known examples are the *chaubara* in Bidar and the Char Minar in Hyderabad; and less well-known examples can be found at Udgir and at Karempudi, the latter taking the same form as the one at Warangal.

KHUSH MAHAL

Having explored the site of the Svayambhu Shiva complex and paid their respects to the four-faced *linga* in the nearby Shambhuni Gudi courtyard, the visitor should then walk 160 metres west to inspect the comparatively well-preserved, monumental stone audience hall erected by the Tughluq governor of Warangal, known as the Khush Mahal. (To gain entry, one should retain the ticket purchased for the Svayambhu Shiva archaeological zone.)

Khush Mahal, exterior; see also photograph on page 20

From the **exterior**, the Khush Mahal exudes a sense of military strength and majesty, in part thanks to its massive, slightly sloping walls, a feature typical of Tughluq style architecture. The rest of the governor's palace must have been located around this imposing structure, but was perhaps built of wood and other less permanent materials. The audience hall is entered from the north through a nesting series of three diminishing transverse arches. These would have had the effect of visually framing the governor or his representative enthroned in state on a raised platform at the southern end of the hall.

The **interior** of the Khush Mahal is roofed with a wooden ceiling (rebuilt in the early 2000s after many years of being open-roofed) carried on seven transverse arches. These exhibit pointed, slightly horseshoe profiles, which are another typical Tughluq stylistic feature. In the middle of the hall is a sunken rectangular pool, which would have been fed by water channels below the pavement coming from the Shringara Bavi, a rectangular tank located some 60 metres directly north of the hall. There is even some evidence of a gravity-fed fountain or fountains in the central pool. On each of the long sides of the hall, light from the six arched doorways and surmounting clerestory windows would have suffused the structure.

Until recently, this structure was popularly known as Shitab Khan's Hall, which has led to its being misdated to the early 16th century. But the unmistakable Tughluq stylistic features just noticed, together with the similarity of conception between its longitudinal, northward orientation and that of the only slightly earlier Tughluq audience hall in Tughluqabad in Delhi, make a much stronger case for its early 14th-century date, and for its construction under the patronage of Muhammad bin Tughluq. If this dating and attribution are correct, then Warangal's Khush Mahal provides an important transitional architectural link between Tughluq Delhi and the earliest Bahmani buildings in the Deccan, like those at Daulatabad and Gulbarga. It would also happen to be the best-preserved example of the longitudinal audience hall to have survived from anywhere in the extensive domains of the Delhi Sultanate.

Khush Mahal,
interior

EASTERN GATEWAY OF THE FORT

Doubling back and descending from Ekashila hill, and turning right onto the main eastern road, the visitor will encounter little of archaeological interest until reaching the stone-clad wall of Warangal Fort and its main **eastern gateway**. The defensive nature of the city's inner stone gateways may best be appreciated by exiting through this best-preserved of the four gates, and then turning around and moving gradually through it. As one approaches the wall from outside the fort, the massive gatehouse looms up above the moat and projects outward some 55 metres from the curtain wall. The roadway approaches and then turns sharply left, as the entrance is on the flank of the gatehouse; this is designed to make the members of an attacking army expose their unshielded right sides as they approach. Once the invaders had turned to face the outermost door, they would have had to withstand a rain of arrows launched by defenders on the battlements above the door and flanking buttresses, as well as from guards stationed atop the curving barbican wall behind them. Should they gain entrance, then the invaders would have had to proceed between two raised guard platforms at ground level, and be subjected to more arrows shot from the battlements above on all sides as they moved through the rectangular outer court. Arriving at the far end, they had to turn again to face the door – this time to the left. If they succeeded in gaining entry through this second door, they still faced an even larger and more open courtyard to be crossed before they arrived at the final door to the city at the innermost end.

The visitor should be sure to notice a pair of **sculpted *yalis***, the horned, leonine creatures placed on the ground outside the outermost of the three doors, flanking the entrance to the gateway. Carved from pink granite, they were originally intended to function as balustrades for a stairway. The *yali* prances forward but turns its head backwards, and a long, abstracted octagonal-sectioned lotus stem issues from its mouth and cascades downward, delimiting the upper curving surface of the stairway. The two balustrades must once have flanked a stairway providing

PREVIOUS PAGES Western gateway to Warangal Fort

BELOW Sculpted *yali* balustrade in the eastern gateway

access to a *mandapa* of some major temple within the city, most likely the Svayambhu Shiva itself. Interestingly, while there is a second pair of identical *yali* balustrades in an analogous position at the stone gateway in the western wall of Warangal Fort, there are none at either the northern or the southern gateways. Reinforcing this pattern of east-west emphasis is a free-standing, curved barbican wall outside each of the western and eastern gateways, but not at either the northern or southern gateways. All of this suggests that when these features were added in the 15th and 16th centuries, the eastern and western gates were more important and heavily trafficked than those to the north and south. The present-day settlement within Warangal Fort also follows this pattern, with the bulk of houses clustered along the east-west road or the small lanes that branch off from it.

Curved barbican wall outside the western gateway in the second ring of walls of of Warangal Fort

VENKATESHVARA TEMPLE

The visitor should be encouraged to seek out two other structures of very different character in the northeast quadrant of Warangal Fort. By turning to the right inside the eastern gateway and following the curving

Venkateshvara Temple, view and vestibule doorway

road that runs around the base of the stone wall, and then proceeding northward for about 70 metres, one will encounter a dirt path. This turns off to the northwest and runs past several present-day buildings devoted to agricultural processing. This path issues forth into agricultural fields, towards a temple structure standing within a rectangular enclosure wall. Since the path soon peters out, the visitor must tread carefully on the earthen field boundaries.

Today popularly known as the **Venkateshvara temple**, this somewhat remotely situated monument was in the early decades of the 16th century known as the temple of Panchaliraya. A form of Krishna, Panchaliraya takes his name from the epic heroine Draupadi (also known as Panchali), who worshipped him when the evil Kauravas were disrobing her in public. Although the temple looks at first glance like a Kakatiya period structure, and indeed is built almost entirely from Kakatiya components, these genuine parts are combined in such a way that they violate standard Kakatiya stylistic syntax. This can be seen most vividly in the doorway leading into the temple vestibule. Thus, the doorframe at first appears to be divided into the standard projecting bands of vegetal stalks and jewelled bands. On closer inspection, however, it is apparent

that the jambs of the doorframe are in fact made from two ornate Kakatiya ceiling beams that have been split lengthwise to create a total of four jamb components placed side by side to create mirror images of each other. The original components have been rotated 90 degrees in order to work in their new locations, and as a result some of the decorative festoons appear to defy gravity by projecting inward rather than hanging downward. Traces of the splitting can be seen on the rear faces of the split jambs, and also along the inner surface of the door passageway, where it is clear that the lotus rosettes that would originally have projected from the undersides of the beams, have been chiselled off to make the reused parts more appropriate for their new locations. Throughout the temple, especially in the pillars of the mandapa and in the slabs of the outer wall of the sanctuary, are analogous instances where genuine Kakatiya components have been creatively re-employed in unusual ways.

It has recently been suggested that this structure may be identified as the temple of Panchaliraya mentioned in a foundation inscription issued in 1504 by Shitab Khan. This Persianised Telugu warrior had served for some years at the Bahmani court but had then left to make his own bid for political supremacy. One crucial key to his strategy was to capitalize on the still vital memory of the Kakatiyas by occupying Warangal and re-consecrating three prominent Kakatiya deities, one of whom was Panchaliraya. Since Panchaliraya's original Kakatiya temple was no longer standing, however, he first had to collect and assemble fragments from this and other Kakatiya period structures. The precise parts needed for this project were not readily available, so the architects had to be highly creative in finding ways to improvise and make scarce parts go around.

Returning to the road at the base of the wall, and continuing for 500 metres northwards and westwards, the visitor will see a rectangular structure in the fields a short distance from the wall. Built of mortared stone masonry, it has a plan of two-by-five bays. Each bay is defined by four square-sectioned piers supporting pointed arches, which in turn carry a groin-vaulted ceiling. All of the outer arches except the middle one on each of the two long sides have been filled in with masonry of the same fabric as the structural parts. It has been suggested that this 15th- or 16th-century building may be identified as a stables. However, the steps and high thresholds of the two doorways suggest that it would

Ruined granary

more likely have served as a **granary**. It is in fact of a form typical of granaries of this period.

GRANARY, KONDA MASJID AND MADELANNA GUDI

Visitors should be encouraged to inspect several buildings of interest in the southwest quadrant of Warangal Fort. The first of these to be described is another **granary** located some 150 metres north-northwest from the southern gateway. This takes the form of three parallel rectangular halls, with their longitudinal axes running east to west, and with sufficient space between them for air circulation. The halls are situated atop an elevated sheetrock outcrop, which would have promoted drainage away from the structures. The open sheetrock area surrounding the halls would have provided ample workspace for threshing and winnowing the grain before taking it inside. In fact, there are hundreds of grinding slicks worn into the sheetrock around the structures, such as would have been produced by hulling and polishing grain. Structurally, the buildings combine rubble masonry and timber construction. No wooden members are preserved, but recessed, empty channels in the masonry reveal where they were once placed. This

timbered, masonry type of structure may occasionally be found in Bahmani-period structures, but apparently not later. Similar examples are seen at Golconda and at Bhongir.

Also in the southwest quadrant of Warangal Fort is an early mosque of architectural importance, known as the **Konda Masjid**. It may be reached from the Svayambhu Shiva complex by walking south on the main southern road for 150 metres and following the road when it turns to the right. After walking another 300 metres or so to the west, the visitor will see the mosque on the left, behind several houses, but still visible from the road. Like the collapsed Jami Masjid on the Svayambhu Shiva site, this too may be assigned to Tughluq patronage, but it likely postdates the Tughluq congregational mosque by about a decade or so. This is because it showcases a new style of architecture that does not reuse dismantled temple materials, and confidently employs imported Islamic structural forms such as brickwork arches and domes.

The **mosque interior** is three bays deep by thirteen bays long, from north to south. Only the six southernmost rows of bays are fully preserved; in the next five bays the structure is gone but the *qibla* wall at the rear of the mosque is still present, while in the northernmost two bays nothing is left except the plinth. Each bay is defined by four stone columns with plain square-sectioned shafts, each shaft standing on a square stone base and carrying a capital that flares out toward the bottom. The pointed arches have horseshoe profiles (thanks to the flaring capitals), but are somewhat squatter than those employed in the *mihrab* and the *minbar* of the Jami Masjid of the Svayambhu Shiva site, or in the interior of the Khush Mahal. The dome above each bay is flat and compressed, made from brick and mortar, with the zone of transition alternating between stretcher courses and courses with the bricks set at an angle so as to create a zipper-like pattern. The *qibla* wall is made of large ashlar slabs and has three *mihrabs*, in the third, seventh, and eleventh bays. Each *mihrab* consists of an outer and inner nested arch, with a smaller blind arch at the back wall, with pendant lotus buds along the arch's inner profile. The pilasters carrying these arches belong to the same Delhi-inspired order as is seen in the *mihrab* and *minbar* fragments of the Jami Mosque.

Returning to the road and continuing northwestward 250 metres, the road junctions with the main east-west road. Continuing

Konda Masjid, dilapidated prayer hall with *qibla* wall

westward on this road for 100 metres, the visitor comes to the western gateway of Warangal Fort. Turning right and following the path that runs around the walls for another 300 metres, one will pass a temple with a nine-bayed *mandapa* and then notice a small temple in the fields just 20 metres away. While not an imposing edifice, this second temple – known as **Madelanna Gudi** – is exceptionally well-preserved, and may well be the clearest example of a Phamsana mode temple anywhere in the Kakatiya dominions. Consisting of just a sanctuary and vestibule, the walls are plain ashlar from ground up to the entablature, which consists of a plain lintel, an overhanging eave and a roll cornice. Above the entablature, the superstructure rises up in six more levels, each consisting of a cornice above a necking recess, and each smaller than the one beneath it. This stepped pyramidal mass carries a square-to-dome tower above a recessed necking. The roughly carved portion on its east side indicates that there would originally have been a barrel-vaulted projection over the vestibule; unfortunately this is no longer preserved.

PALAMPET

THE RECHERLA REDDIS

Leaving the Kakatiyas' own crown lands around Hanamkonda and Warangal, we now move some 60 kilometres northeast to Palampet and Ghanpur, in the core territories of the lineage of Kakatiya feudatories known as the Recherla Reddis. By Kakatiya Ganapatideva's reign, the Recherlas had been serving the Kakatiyas already for five generations, since the time of their ancestor Bamma Senani, who had been a military officer under Kakatiya Beta I. Recherla Rudra Reddi, also known as Rudra Senapati ("General Rudra"), became one of the most trusted generals under Ganapatideva, and even appears to have taken the reins of government for a few years when Ganapatideva was being held in captivity by the Yadavas.

Recherla Rudra is credited with founding a city known as Atukuru (present-day Palampet), which is described in a contemporary inscription as "brilliantly shooting up lofty pinnacles, in which are delightful palaces, and constant fortunes of every kind" (see Appendix No. 4). Although the further comparisons made with the cities of various epic heroes – Ayodhya, Mathura, and so on – confirm one's sense that this is largely hyperbole, Atukuru in its day must nonetheless have been an impressive town. In addition to the monumental architecture of its temples, there was another landmark associated with the accomplished Rudra Senapati. This is **Ramappa lake**, the vast *cheruvu* that he created by having a 600-metre-long dam constructed between two adjacent ridges. The water impounded in this reservoir stretches today 5 kilometers wide and 2 kilometres long and irrigates an area of almost 2,000 hectares. According to the Ramappa temple inscription, the irrigation tank "stands like an ocean that has come thither from fear of the Submarine Fire, and looks like a mirror for that city... all the clouds certainly take up its water, and not that of the ocean, for they everywhere carry sweet water, not salty" (Appendix No. 5).

See photograph on page 119

The inscription goes on to tell us that in the year 1213 CE, **Recherla Rudra** established a temple in Atukuru and dedicated it to the god Rudreshvara. Known today as Ramappa, this is without doubt the grandest and most impressive of all Kakatiya temples to be seen today. In addition to this monument, there are at least another seven smaller temples scattered around the site, in various states of preservation and with varying degrees of architectural interest. Collectively, the temples

Ramappa Temple

PREVIOUS PAGES Interior of *ranga-mandapa* of main temple

OPPOSITE Stone stele in the courtyard with the foundation inscription of Recherla Rudra at Palampet have justly been described by Yazdani, as "among the brightest stars in the galaxy of medieval Deccan temples". Two distinct factors account for Yazdani's superlative evaluation. First, the Ramappa is perhaps the most complete Kakatiya temple complex, featuring the full range of structures, from primary and secondary temples to the surrounding enclosure wall articulated with an *asthana-mandapa* (currently dismantled in preparation for reassembly). In the intervening space are various specialized structures, such as the Nandi pavilion, an inscription pavilion, and an enclosed room with an open porch that may have served as a kitchen for preparation of the ritual offerings for the deities. Second, it is the most perfectly preserved Kakatiya monument, with its brick tower fully intact and even with the majority of its delicate bracket figures still in place around the *ranga-mandapa.*

The Ramappa temple exemplifies the **local stylistic idiom** of the northeastern region of Warangal District, then known as Polavasa-desha. One factor contributing to the distinctiveness of this architectural style was the exclusive use of locally available pink sandstone as the main building material, in place of the granite used in the metropolitan style of Warangal. In the largest temples at Palampet, however, black dolerite was still employed for the main structural elements, such as the columns and beams of the central bay, thereby achieving a pleasing juxtaposition of color and texture between the two types of stone.

RAMAPPA TEMPLE

Recherla Rudra Reddi's temple is today approached from the west, via a path that leads through a garden to a poorly preserved doorway in the enclosure wall that defines the **temple precinct**. This doorway

Ramappa Temple, view of main shrine (**RIGHT**) and Gaurisha Temple (**LEFT**)

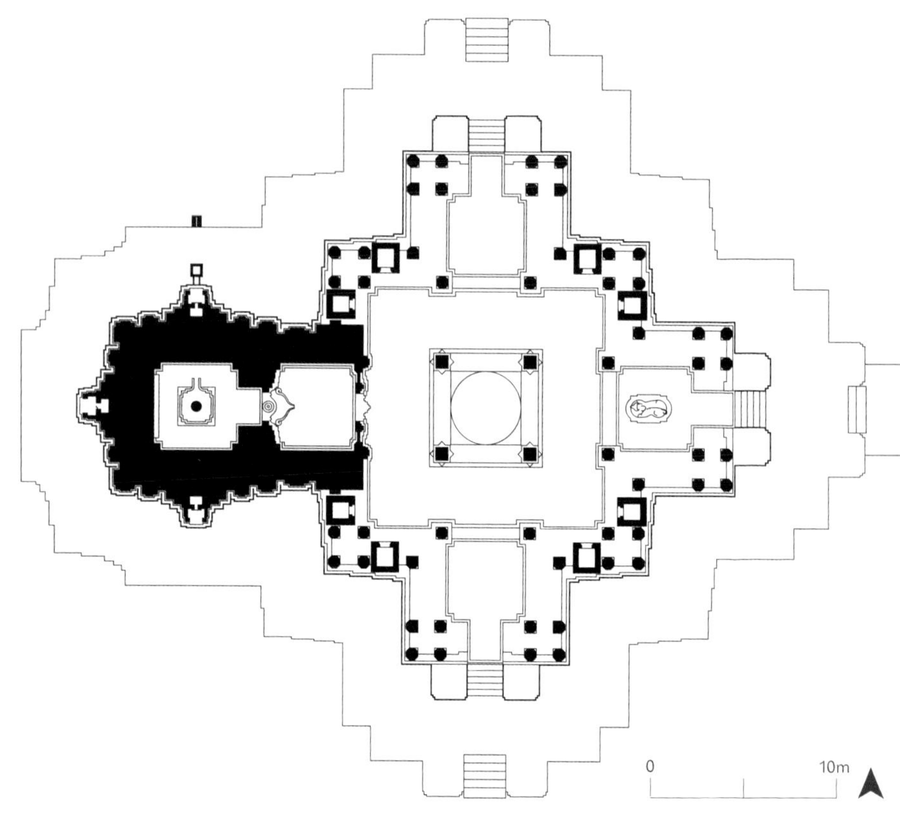

retains only its right-hand doorjamb; that on the left and the original lintel above are missing. The doorway on the opposite side of the enclosure is fully intact. Because it opens into the enclosure at a point directly on axis with the Nandi pavilion and the main temple, this eastern doorway was probably conceived as one of two originally intended points of entry to the temple, the other being the *asthana-mandapa* that is articulated with the enclosure wall on the south.

Some 2.7 metres high, the **enclosure wall** is made from finely dressed inner and outer stone shells filled with rubble, and capped by horizontal slabs overhanging slightly on each side. As originally constructed, the wall carried a continuous course of spade-shaped merlons along the outer side, although these are now preserved only in several places, most notably along the south.

Entering the compound from the west, the visitor first encounters the rear of the **main temple**, which looms up straight ahead and to the right. It is a single-shrined temple with a well-preserved tower containing a sanctuary and vestibule facing east. It is fronted by an imposing, attached *ranga-mandapa* with projecting porches to north, east, and south; in front of the eastern porch is an impressive Nandi pavilion. The entire ensemble stands on an elevated and broad platform that provides ample space for open-air circumambulation. The only way to access the platform is via stairways in front of the north and south porches of the *ranga-mandapa*, and by a pair of stairways along the sides of the raised causeway connecting the Nandi pavilion to the *ranga-mandapa* on the east. Pairs of carved stone elephants, some better preserved than others, flank each stairway where it emerges at the top of the platform.

Ramappa Temple

OPPOSITE Plan of main shrine

BELOW Nandi pavilion

It is recommended that the visitor proceed eastward and first climb the stairs in front of the **Nandi pavilion**. This structure is roughly square in plan, but with projections on the west to accommodate the stairways through its platform and its plinth. It takes the form of an open-aired, single-bay *mandapa*, with its roof – now missing – originally carried on four half-columns rising up from the corners of the seat slabs atop its half-walls. It is surrounded on all sides by a high seatback that breaks only at the entrance to the pavilion, where the ends of its slabs are carved with Shaiva door-guardians. The seatback is is lavishly carved with diamond-shaped flowers, musicians and dancers, and most notably, a frieze

Ramappa Temple

ABOVE Nandi

OPPOSITE Relief carvings on the shrine walls

of elephants processing in a clockwise direction, paying their respects to Shiva's bull. Carved out of beautifully detailed and polished black dolerite, the Nandi inside sits facing west toward his lord venerated in the sanctuary. Outside, on the northern side, a drain-spout projects from the floor level of the pavilion and channels the water used to lustrate Nandi through a hollow column and into a second spout at plinth level. This shows clearly that Nandi was also intended to receive worship.

Following Nandi's gaze and turning westward toward the main Ramappa temple, the visitor should follow the steps down from the pavilion and across the causeway and then up again to the **temple platform**. Instead of going straight up the steps and in to the *ranga-mandapa*, one should walk clockwise around the platform, following the direction of the elephant frieze that will be just about at eye-level to the viewer's right. These elephants may all appear similar at first, but soon one realizes that they are carved with subtle differences and contrasting gaits, some looking forward and others turning their heads back, some

grabbing human attendants in their trunks, and so on. Periodically, at key intervals, a pair of elephants lustrating a deity with their elevated trunks interrupts the motion – in several cases it is, appropriately, the elephant-headed god Ganesha who is thus honoured. The visitor should be sure to stop to closely observe the ornate precision of the carving of the three-storeyed miniature shrines projecting from the midpoints of the sanctuary wall. Intricately conceived and precisely executed, these shrines are complete with doorways, ceiling panels, and even sockets for bracket figures (now unfortunately missing).

At some point in their circumambulation, the visitor should move out to the edge of the platform, or down to the level of the ground on the south side, so as to get an idea of the overall **elevation** of the Ramappa temple. This presents the clearest example of the Vesara mode in all of Kakatiya architecture. The sanctuary is divided by recesses into five projecting sections on each side, the edges of each projection articulated by a pair of plain but gracefully attenuated pilasters. These carry an entablature featuring most prominently an enormous projecting eave with an intricately carved underside mimicking a wooden structure. In many places, this preserves its original painted decoration. Within each pair of pilasters on the wall projections is a shrine model consisting of a pair of pilasters carrying a miniature Dravida-type tower, recognized by pyramidal, superimposed "storeys" capped with a square-to-dome roof. A contrasting shrine model with a schematized Phamsana-type tower carried on a single pilaster rising from a pot is seen within each recess. Close inspection reveals that these single pilasters are framed by half-pilasters carrying *makara-toranas* in the form of a lotus scroll arch issuing from an aquatic creature's mouth on each side. Finally, the central projection of each side is divided into a main face and two secondary projections on each side. This five-part division of the central projection thus recapitulates the five-part rhythm of the larger temple itself, thus contributing to the tight integration of its overall design.

The wall divisions of the ground storey of the Ramappa temple carry on up into the well-preserved Vesara **tower**, consisting of another three compressed storeys capped by a square-to-dome roof, surmounted by a golden pot finial. Although compacted, these upper storeys can still be visually resolved into abbreviated wall sections, showing the same five-fold rhythm of the projections framed by pilasters established in the ground floor.

Ramappa Temple

OPPOSITE Three-storey shrine projection in the south sanctuary walls; see also photograph on page 25

FOLLOWING PAGES View of *ranga-mandapa* from the east, and details of figural brackets; see photographs on pages 4-5

PALAMPET

PALAMPET

The parapet course above is divided into small shrine models aligned over each projection of the wall. The resulting effect is one of a perfectly stable harmony between vertical and horizontal lines of composition.

(The visitor will notice thin piers composed of mortared sandstone blocks, some placed between the sculpted bracket figures. These are not original features of the temple, but were inserted by Yazdani to prop up the wide projecting eave that runs continuously around the hall. The same is true of the parapet wall atop the hall.)

Before entering the temple, the visitor should do one more round of circumambulation outside, this time to marvel at the splendid sculpted **bracket figures** of the *ranga-mandapa*, for which the Ramappa is so famous. These brackets are of two kinds: nearly human-size figures of female dancers, musicians, and goddesses, placed in groups of four supporting the edges of the eaves over the outer face of each porch, and in all other portions of the eaves, mythical *yalis* attacking elephants. Both kinds of brackets have tenons in their bases and in their tops, which are fitted into sockets on the column shafts and the edges of the eave, respectively.

The female bracket figures are quite distinctive on account of their exaggeratedly slender proportions and their highly polished finish, giving them an almost metallic sheen. Some appear to be the work of less experienced sculptors, but others, charged with energy and torsion, are clearly the work of an accomplished master. According to Yazdani: "the suggestion of movement and pulsating life conveyed by the gestures of fingers and the poses of the bodies appeals to the artistic sense, more particularly because the sculptor has managed to give a wonderful impression of youth and rhythm. The outline of the body seems to move in curves, indicating in each pose, or dancing-step, an emotional grace and a mood of exultation seldom to be met with in Indian sculpture of the earlier periods".

After admiring the various bracket figures, the visitor should enter the **interior** of the *ranga-mandapa* through one of its three stairways. Atop each stairway, passage is provided through the half-walls, and the ends of the seat-back slabs on either side are sculpted with images of female figures, portrayed standing under a natural framing arch of banana trees and creeping vines. While its layout and overall form are reminiscent of that of the Thousand-Pillared Temple at Hanamkonda, the Ramappa temple *mandapa* is considerably larger, and stylistically more mannered and ornate. Because of its greater size, the half-columns on the half-wall rise up in

PREVIOUS PAGES AND ABOVE
Ramappa Temple columns in the *ranga-mandapa*

square groupings of four instead of singly, as at Hanamkonda, and at the recessed inner angles between *ranga-mandapa* and porch, the columns are arranged in pairs along a diagonal line. These carry both an inner and an outer circuit of beams. Another notable difference is that small secondary shrines have been erected on the seat-slabs of the half-wall of the *ranga-mandapa*, two in every corner for a total of eight. These all have miniature doorways and some still contain sculpted images of various subsidiary deities, including Ganesha, Vishnu, Sarasvati, and Durga slaying the buffalo demon. As at Hanamkonda, the central bay is the main focus, featuring black dolerite components within the larger matrix of pink sandstone: notably, the four central columns, the beams and ceiling slabs they carry, and the raised circular podium on the floor in between. These black dolerite accents continue in the doorframes of the vestibule and sanctuary, and in the beautifully preserved Rudreshvara *linga* and its pedestal.

Although only some 50 years separate the Ramappa from the Hanamkonda monument, the **sculpted ornament** at Palampet now encrusts almost every component of the four central columns, and all three sides of the ceiling beams are carved with narrative friezes relating various episodes from the mythology of Shiva. These include, among others, a memorable tableau of Shiva's slaying of Gajasura, in which Shiva dances inside the flayed skin of the elephant demon, and his slaying of the demons of the Three Cities, in which the demons are shown worshipping the Jain Tirthankara Parshvanatha. There are also more auspicious scenes, including the churning of the cosmic ocean, in which the gods gained the nectar of immortality, and the marriage of Shiva and Parvati. Of equal interest are the inventive ceiling panels of the eight peripheral bays surrounding the central bay. These take the form of three-tiered lantern ceilings, with bisected floral motifs in each triangular corner slab, and then one of a variety of different motifs in the central slab. In some bays, the central slab is sculpted as a multi-ringed lotus and in others, it is carved in the form of a corbelled ribbed dome. In one compelling design used in several bays, two concentric interlaced strapwork squares are arranged to make an eight-pointed star, and eight smaller stars are arranged around the central one, with *kirti-mukha* monster-masks filling up the triangular space in the corners. This design is intriguingly reminiscent of the *girih* mode of Islamic ornament, likewise based on star motifs with overlaid strapwork, which first appeared in the middle east about a century and half before the date of the Ramappa temple.

See photograph on pages 6-7

FOLLOWING PAGES Ramappa Temple, *ranga-mandapa* ceiling

Ramappa Temple, ceiling

The visitor to Palampet should not neglect the other structures in the Ramappa enclosure. The smaller, Bhumija-type structure just north of the main temple is almost certainly the **Gaurisha temple**, which Recherla Rudra mentions together with Rudreshvara in his foundation inscription. It uses no dolerite and is constructed entirely from pink sandstone. As in the main temple, recesses divide the shrine walls into five projecting sections on each side. Here, however, each projecting member is given the form of a single pilaster, which is in keeping with

the Bhumija mode. Traces of the first level of the Bhumija superstructure can be made out above the walls. A square-planned, nine-bayed *mandapa* on the front is open-sided, with half-walls topped with seat-slabs and back-rests, carved with friezes on the exterior. It has no porches on any side, the only access to the interior being via a single flight of stairs on the eastern side. Inside the *mandapa*, diminutive stone shrines are (or were) found on the seat slabs of the half-wall, three each along the northern and southern sides, and only two on the east and west.

Gaurisha Temple; see also photograph on page 22

OPPOSITE
Pavilion with stone stele inscribed by Recherla Rudra

In between the Ramappa and the Gaurisha temples, and displaced somewhat toward the east, is a small **single-bayed pavilion** housing the monumental stele on which is carved Recherla Rudra's foundation inscription (see Appendix No. 5).

The ***asthana-mandapa*** of the Ramappa complex is situated directly on axis with the entrance of the *ranga-mandapa* of the main temple. This imposing structure has now been dismantled in preparation for conservation work, and all of its constituent parts are lying in piles outside the temple enclosure on north and south. Its design was similar to that of the *asthana-mandapa* at Hanamkonda, featuring a central, square space enclosed by solid walls, with four sets of four columns supporting the ceiling beams, doorways on the north and south, and balconies on the east and west. Yet it departs from that earlier precedent in being raised on a doubled supporting terrace. It is also noteworthy that the enclosure wall articulates with the *asthana-mandapa* by extending over the two platforms and abutting the southern ends of the lateral porches. As a result, most of the structure is contained within the sacred precinct.

OTHER TEMPLES

The visitor should be encouraged to visit three other temples at Palampet of varying degrees of interest and states of preservation, despite their relative inaccessibility. These can be combined and visited in a walk of about one kilometre ending at the great Ramappa *cheruvu*. Leaving the Ramappa compound and walking west to the road running between the village and the lake, and then turning left toward the lake, within a very short distance one will see a small temple on the right, behind a house and surrounded at the time of this writing by vegetable gardens. It is a nameless, **single-shrined temple**, consisting only of a sanctuary preceded by a vestibule. The temple is built in the Phamsana mode, and features plain masonry walls articulated with a faint buttress projecting ever so slightly from the plane of the corner pilasters. Atop the projecting eaves of the entablature rises an eight-tiered superstructure ending in an upturned cornice surmounted by a square-to-dome roof. A gable projecting out from the fabric of the tower roofs the vestibule. What is especially noteworthy about this unassuming building is that its tower manifests a gracefully curvilinear profile, and displays a central projecting spine running up the middle of each side, two features that reveal the

ABOVE AND OPPOSITE Palampet, Golla Gudi, view and corbelled ceiling

heritage of the northern Indian Nagara tradition of temple architecture. Although locally referred to as Shiva temple (one of several in this vicinity), its southern orientation suggests that the temple might in fact have been dedicated to the worship of Vishnu, who commonly faces in this direction in Telangana temples during the Kakatiya period. Though of uncertain date, the temple may be the earliest structure surviving at Palampet, belonging to the latter half of the 12th century.

Continuing down the road a short distance, the visitor will notice to the left a partially dilapidated triple-shrined temple, locally known as **Golla Gudi**, standing at the edge of irrigated rice paddies and surrounded by coconut trees. It is a gem of a temple and well worth a look inside. It is oriented to the east, and originally housed three Shiva *lingas*, which suggests that it was perhaps a commemorative monument. Its three shrines are all Phamsana mode and have plain

masonry walls; unfortunately the towers over the sanctuaries are no longer preserved. Stylistically, the temple appears to be datable to the mid-13th century. Yet, it shows a number of archaizing features, such as the vestibules that are completely open at the front without any doorframes or even *makara-toranas*, and the higher elevation of the ceiling of the central *mandapa* bay, and the diagonally down-sloping ceilings of the surrounding bays. Other notable attributes include the elaborately carved corbelled ceiling of the central bay of the *mandapa*, which rises up in the form of a square dome with pendant cusps, and the inventive and well-executed sculpted treatment of its external wall. Unlike the *mandapas* of the other temples considered in this guidebook, this hall is completely enclosed, except that instead of having solid walls, it features carved lattice screens inserted in between "false" columns rising from the tops of the back-rest seating slabs. The underside of the widely projecting eave is carved with forms that hark back to wooden-frame antecedents, and does so with greater detail and complexity than any other documented Kakatiya temple. The eminent architectural historian M.A. Dhaky believed that this temple was perhaps constructed by a different guild of artisans from those who worked on the Ramappa and other temples at Palampet, and held that its sensitive craftsmanship was unprecedented in medieval Telangana. It would be an ideal candidate for some judicious repair and conservation work.

Continuing the rest of the way down the road to the **Ramappa lake**, the road will begin to climb the lower flank of the hill on the right, affording the visitor with views of the verdant rice fields to the left of the road. All of this green land is irrigated by the water of the reservoir, fed out through a network of canals, many of which date back to the time of Recherla Rudra's original benefaction. The road finally ends at a junction with the road that runs along the top of the tank *bund*, from which one can enjoy a fine panorama of the reservoir, especially towards sunset.

After taking in the fresh breezes from the lake, the visitor should head toward the west end of the tank *bund*, on which is located the third temple described here. This is another **triple-shrined temple**, and like the previous one, it too is oriented to the east. It accommodates three Shiva *lingas*, and is built in the Phamsana mode. Though there is nothing remarkable about the temple architecturally, it happens to be of some historical interest. Given the late 12th- or early 13th-century date, and its apparent status as a commemorative triple shrine, it seems possible that this is the temple mentioned in the last verse of Recherla Rudra's inscription (see Appendix 4). There, it is recorded that in addition to making a donation to "the god who is well established in the ever fortunate goodly town of Atukuru [=Palampet]", Rudra also donated the village of Nradkude "to Kateshvara and to Kameshvara, and to Rudreshvara" for their enjoyment. Since Kata[ya] was the name of Rudra's father, and Kama[mbika] the name of his mother, this is clearly a reference to a triple-shrine commemorative monument, with the *lingas* dedicated in the names of his father, his mother, and himself. Although the inscription does not explicitly state that the temple in question was erected in Palampet or "Atukuru", it would appear to be quite likely, and may well have been built at the same time as the establishment of the reservoir itself.

Dam wall of
Ramappa Lake
near Palamapet

GHANPUR

From Palampet, it is only about 9 kilometres northwest to Ghanpur. The town offers an instructive comparison to Palampet, since it also has a vast Kakatiya period *cheruvu* (although not quite as extensive as Palampet's), as well as a large and impressive major temple, the Kota Gudi. Many specific architectural features are shared in common between the Ramappa and Kota Gudi complexes, but there are also noteworthy differences. One is that the Kota Gudi is poorly preserved; even its primary shrine is in woeful condition, having lost the entirety of the roof of its *ranga-mandapa*. Another significant difference is that since no foundation inscription has been discovered there is no information available about who the patron of the temple could have been. Its general similarity with the Ramappa temple suggests that it is roughly contemporaneous; perhaps it was built by another member of the Recherla family who was vying competitively with Rudra Senapati at Palampet. It has been suggested that it may slightly post-date the Ramappa, as it seems to improve upon that temple's plan with respect to the clarity of alignments between its constituent structures.

KOTA GUDI

Like its counterpart at Palampet, the Kota Gudi at Ghanpur is oriented east and occupies a sacred precinct once defined by a rectangular enclosure wall, major parts of which have collapsed and disappeared. Although today the only point of entrance is from the west side, immediately behind the main temple, the original preferred point of entry was evidently through the *asthana-mandapa* articulated with the wall on the south. This is a poorly preserved jumble of pillars and beams, some still standing precariously, but enough survives to demonstrate that the north-south axis of this structure, defined by stairways on each side, continued northward as the entrance axis for the *mandapas* of the primary and secondary temples. This is in contrast to Palampet, where the secondary temple of Gaurisha could only be entered by a stairway on the east, there being no porches or entrances on either the south or the north.

What most distinguishes the Kota Gudi is the group of nineteen **subsidiary shrines** arrayed around the periphery of the sacred space within the enclosure, and oriented with their doorways opening in toward the centre of the precinct. Some shrines are quite well preserved all the way up to the tops of their superstructures, while others remain

PREVIOUS PAGES Reddi Gudi

OPPOSITE Plan of Kota Gudi

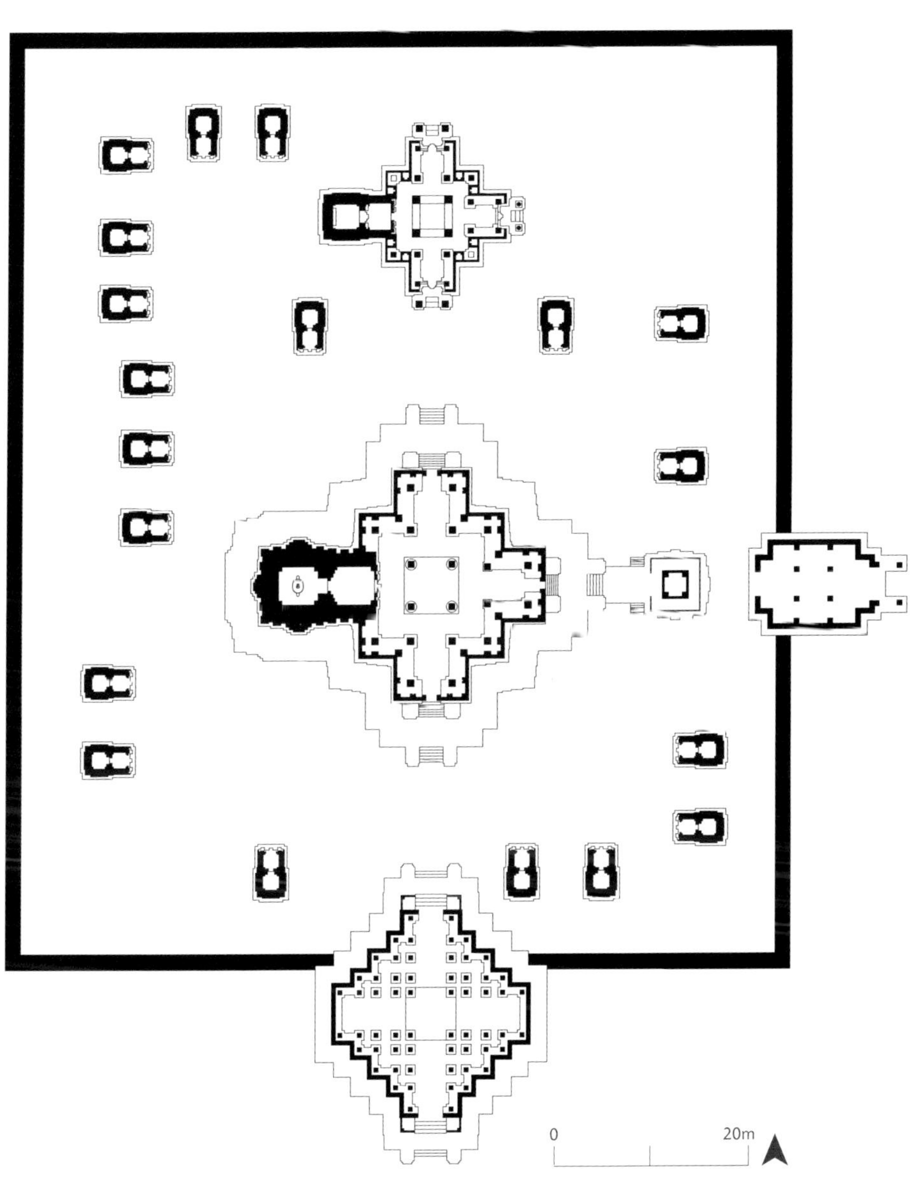

GHANPUR

Kota Gudi, subsidiary shrines

only as foundation traces. They are simple structures consisting only of sanctuaries and vestibules. Although they have plain masonry walls, which would generally suggest the Phamsana mode, in this case they are capped with both Vesara and Bhumija superstructures. The towers of both these types are divided into three upper storeys; those of the Bhumija type have a central spine that runs up to the "bell" in which such superstructures typically end.

The **main temple** of the Kota Gudi is built in the Bhumija mode. Although it has lost its superstructure, this is still clear from the treatment of its wall projections, each carved as a single, broad column. Like the Palampet temple, its shrine is divided into five projections on each side, and it features a prominently projecting eave with an intricately carved and painted undersurface. Although there are places where the sandstone has weathered considerably, many parts of the temple have maintained their crisply realized forms and intricate

Kota Gudi, main temple from the east

decorative details. The *ranga-mandapa* is similar to that at Palampet: it has the same groupings of outer columns in fours and in twos. Additionally, it has the smaller shrine chambers on the seating slabs of the *ranga-mandapa's* half-walls. One striking detail inside is the frieze on the half-wall beneath the seating slabs; this has lotus rosettes divided into sixteen petals, rather than the usual four or eight.

The ***ranga-mandapa*** of the Kota Gudi also originally featured bracket figures analogous to those at Palampet, although only a few have survived due to the collapse of a great portion of the structure. Those that do remain fall into the same two types: composite *yalis*, and women dancing or playing music. What is most striking, however, is how stylistically different these figures are from those at Palampet. Overall, they exhibit more natural bodily proportions; their poses, too, are more balanced, not as vibrant as in the Palampet figures, and their faces appear calmer and more self-contained. This suggests that a guild of sculptors

different from that at Palampet was employed at Ghanpur.

The **secondary temple** to the north of the main temple of the Kota Gudi is much simpler, and seems to have been built in Phamsana mode judging from its plain masonry walls. The tower is lost, but the *ranga-mandapa* with its three projecting porches is noteworthy for the unusually tall seat-backs atop the half-walls, with its three superposed bands of curvilinear Nagara-type temple towers, lotus rosettes, and frieze of geese.

The ***asthana-mandapa*** to the south of the main temple conforms to the same general type found at Hanamkonda and Palampet, but the innovation here was to eliminate the solid wall delineating the central square space. Instead, that wall was replaced by another range of columns just like the others within the building, making for an airier, more open interior space. This should be evident once the current vegetation that has invaded the structure will be brought under control!

REDDI GUDI

See photograph on pages 120-121

The second temple of interest at Ghanpur is a poorly preserved monument standing about 500 metres from the Kota Gudi. Built of sandstone, it is a **single-shrined temple** oriented north and standing on a broad platform. It consists of a sanctuary and vestibule, with the walls divided into five projecting members, with a typical half-walled *ranga-mandapa* with three porches. What makes this unusual temple a work of great creativity and innovation is that the architect has produced a harmonious blending of the forms of two distinct modes, the Bhumija

and the Vesara. This is immediately evident on inspecting the walls. Each projection is articulated not only with a pair of slender, plain pilasters framing the edges, as in the Vesara mode, but also with a single broad column in the intervening space, as in the Bhumija, leaving just enough space between the two elements to accentuate the complex rhythm thus produced. Both the columns and the slender pilasters rise up all the way to bear the weight of the entablature, but the shafts of the pilasters extend further up, since they carry only three diminutive capitals, while the shafts of the broader columns stop sooner, as they carry a succession of four, far more substantial capitals. Thanks to the juxtaposition, the design produces a series of dynamic shifts between horizontal and vertical forces at the upper margins of the wall that is unlike anything else in the Telangana temple tradition.

What form of superstructure had the architect contemplated for this unusual shrine? It could have been either Vesara or Bhumija, or the builder might well have experimented with the same kind of juxtaposition and intertwining of formal systems that is evinced in the treatment of the walls. However its tower would have been realized, the Reddi Gudi is an arresting monument and a testament to the bold creativity of the builders of the local style of the Polavasa-desha region.

OPPOSITE AND ABOVE Kota Gudi, details of *yali* bracket and eave overhang

TEMPLE AT NAINPAK

Temple at Nainpak

A little less than 20 kilometers northwest of Ghanpur is the village of Nainpak, which has a post-Kakatiya monument that is well worth a brief detour before heading back to Warangal. This Vaishnava edifice takes the form of a well-preserved Sarvatobhadra temple consisting simply of a square sanctuary with a doorway on each of the four sides, topped by an impressive, well-preserved Vesara tower. The structure of the walls is stone masonry, but the three-storeyed tower is composed of brick.

The **temple facade** is unlike that of any known Kakatiya monument; the walls are not divided into projections, but instead there is an unarticulated expanse of masonry wall relieved at the centre by a shallow rectangular recess framing the doorway. The doorway is divided into two superimposed openings, a lower one framed by a horizontal lintel, and an upper one in the form of an arched window. The builder has inserted a massive reinforcing lintel above the arch, suggesting that he was not fully familiar with the arched method of construction.

The overall conception of the Nainpak temple is reminiscent of early Bahmani funerary architecture, such as the tombs of Daud Shah Bahmani or of Mujarrad Kamal at Gulbarga, both belonging to the end of the 14th century. This impression is still further reinforced by the monolithic stone dome fitted onto the top of the consecrated image inside the sanctuary. These unusual features suggest that the building must date at the earliest to the late 14th century, or more probably, given its provincial nature, to some time around the middle of the 15th century. Given the imperial pretensions of the Sarvatobhadra temple form, it may be that this post-Kakatiya period structure was founded by Ravu Dharmanayaka, a descendent of Recherla Peda Anapota Nayaka who was ruling the Warangal district in the 1460s Ravu Dharmanayaka has left an inscription at Shayampet, some 35 kilometres southwest of Nainpak, recording his donation of lands for the support of a Vaishnava temple (Tiruvengalanatha) at Macherla in Warangal District.

The **enshrined deity** within the temple is most unusual. It appears to be carved from a single massive boulder of a grey-black stone, apparently in situ. On each of its four sides are carvings of different forms of Vishnu: Rama and Sita together with Lakshmana; Narasimha; Krishna quelling the serpent Kaliya; and Balarama.

Sculpted forms of Vishnu enshrined in the temple at Nainpak

NAINPAK

APPENDICES

No. 1: REPORT OF NARRAIN ROW

Narrain Row was one of some 20 Niyogi brahmans who assisted Colonel Colin Mackenzie in his statistical survey of southern India in the first decades of the 19th century. The following excerpts are from a report he sent to Mackenzie's office in Madras in 1816 from Warangal, where he had been dispatched to collect historical accounts of the region and to document antiquities. He is an astute observer of sculpture, iconography, and the built environment. In this excerpt, he speculates on the early popularity of Jainism in Hanamkonda and its displacement by Shaivism, and discusses the contents of the inscription in front of the Padmakshi temple. More recent epigraphic scholarship has shown that Mailama was the wife of the minister Betana, who served Kakatiya Prola II. (From the British Library, London, Oriental and India Office Collections. European Manuscripts. Mackenzie Collections. Translations, Class XII, Letters and Reports, No. 47.)

[36r.] There are Jaina figures carved on the stones on the hill of Hanamkonda [=Gaggaleya Gutta]; west of this hill is another hill called Padmakshi-konda. In the Pagoda of Padmakshi in like manner are Jaina figures carved. I suppose this place was ruled formerly by Jaina Kings and understand from the aged people of this country that the above Beemarasu was a Jaina King; in some places on the hill of Hanamkonda in the time of the Kakatiya Kings, they raised stone walls for foundation but the work was not finished ...

In the year of Chalukya Vikrama 23d or A.S. 1020 – on the Padmavati Hill south west of Hanamkonda nearst to the Pagoda of Padmavati on a rock was carved a number of Jaina figures besides that there are many Jaina figures in the Pagoda of Padmavati, the Goddess Padmavati was belonging to the Jaina religion formerly, but no Jaina people are at present at Hanamkonda. Bramins worship the deity and people of different sects make their vows to her. The inhabitants of Hanamkonda [38r.] say that the Jainas of the northern and western Countries come and worship this Goddess, there is a stone inscription in front of the Goddess on a black stone with the mixture of Kannada and Sanskrit languages on the top of which was engraved the Jaina figures the contents thereof as follows. –

Kakati Prolaraju (son of Tribhuvanamallaraj [Kakatiya Beta]) fought with various Kings and conquered them and established ten Pagodas. His wife Mailamadevi was faithful to the Jaina Goddess and made the Golden peaks for the Goddess [established the temple Kadalalaya Basadi]. In the year of C.Sk. 42 [Chalukya Vikrama era] in the cycle year Hevalambi [=Saka 1039=1117 CE] on the 15th of Paushya month on Monday in Uttarayana holy day has granted some land under the Tank (which was dug in his name [sic: which was established in her name by her husband Betana]) ...

No. 2: PADMAKSHI'S GIFT TO MADHAVA VARMAN

This narrative comes from Prataparudra Charitramu, *a retrospective Telugu prose history of the Kakatiyas, culminating in the reign of Prataparudra, authored in Warangal in about 1550 by one Ekamranatha. The work is an intriguing blend of history, myth, and legend, and incorporates numerous stories from local folklore and traditions. This account attests to the importance of the Padmakshi cult at Hanamkonda, and recounts a popular tradition holding that Madhava Varman, the lineage's legendary founder, received a magic sword and a shield from the goddess Padmakshi, which would enable him and his descendants to rule for 1,000 years. (Translated from C. V. Ramachandra Rao, ed.,* Ekamranathuni Prataparudra Caritramu, *Hyderabad, 1984, pp. 10-11.)*

One day, in his haste to go and play with his schoolmates after their lessons in the Padmakshi temple, young Madhava Varman forgot his slate and books. Unwittingly leaving them near Padmakshi's image, he left the temple and closed the door, and then lost himself in his games with his friends. It was not until after he had gone home and finished his bath and his dinner that he realized he had forgotten his books and slate. Since he would need them later on that evening for his lesson with Madhava Sharma, who would no doubt chastise him for his negligence, he decided to go back and get them. Even though it was nighttime, he slipped out by himself and headed for the temple.

There at the temple, the goddess Padmakshi was sitting in state on her throne, attended by a horde of terrifying demons – there were spirits and ghosts, goblins, sakinis and dhakinis, vampires, and brahma-rakshasas. Without feeling the least bit of fear of this dreadful host, Madhava Varman walked right up to the goddess and picked up his books and slate.

The goddess was surprised to see the boy standing there so fearlessly and decided to test him to see just how brave he really was: in an instant, she assumed her most hideous and frightful form. But the boy just stood there, not the least bit frightened to see her like this, and instead he only folded his hands and began to sing her praise. He prostrated himself before her feet and lay there without standing up. Seeing this, the goddess' heart began to overflow with feelings of affection for the boy, and she said: 'Stand up, dear boy. I appreciate your display of courage and devotion! Ask for a boon, whatever you may please.'

Madhava Varman had learned from his mother of his father's death at the hands of the lord of Cuttack, and so he asked the goddess: 'Please grant me the ability to vanquish the Lord of Cuttack and to get our royal herds back.'

The goddess replied: 'So be it.' She presented the boy with a divine sword and shield, and proclaimed: 'With this sword you shall repel all the enemies who attack you, and by the power of this shield neither swords nor arrows shall reach you. With them you shall rule for two thousand months.' Then, pointing out the mouth of a nearby cave, she added: 'Go westward into that cave. After walking some distance, you will come out of the cave and find yourself in a beautiful place. From that time until sunrise tomorrow, an entire army will issue forth from the cave to serve you.'

Padmakshi continued: 'With this divine sword and shield, your family will occupy the throne for one thousand years. So go and rule the earth, and do not forget to honour cows and brahmins and to offer worship to Uma and Maheshvara and Lakshmi and Narayana!'

The boy bowed to the goddess again and again, and then, he went into the cave as she had instructed. He beheld many threatening obstacles inside, from ghosts and spirits and vampires, to tigers, wolves, and snakes. But he went past them all without letting them shake his resolve, and soon enough he came out of the cave on the other side. He went on for a short distance, and then stopped and stood waiting in that pleasant place.

Just then, a great host of elephants, horses, and heroic foot-soldiers began to issue forth from the cave behind him. They continued coming until sunrise, and the sounds of the assembling army filled all the four quarters. With the booming of kettledrums, the trumpeting of horns, the blowing of conch-trumpets, the jingling of camel bells, the din of chariot wheels, and the varied noises of horses, elephants, and vehicles all mixed together, it was as deafening as the roaring thunder of the great deluge that marks the end of time. Altogether, that magical army amounted to 60,000 rutting elephants, twelve lakhs of the best horses, and seventeen lakhs of foot soldiers. Madhava Varman assembled them all, and collected ten crores of gold pieces, and divine, jewel-encrusted ornaments, and then he returned to his house.

No. 3: THE FOUNDING OF THE CITY OF WARANGAL

This episode, also from the Prataparudra Charitramu *of Ekamranatha, recounts the story of Warangal's founding as a result of the self-manifestation of the god Svayambhu Shiva. Chronologically, this event is ascribed to the reign of Prola II, the father of Rudradeva, but this is clearly earlier than is attested in contemporary inscriptions that date the event to the late 12th century during Rudradeva's reign. (Translated from C. V. Ramachandra Rao, ed.,* Ekamranathuni Prataparudra Caritramu, *Hyderabad, 1984, pp. 23-24.)*

One day when Kakati Prolaraju was ruling the kingdom, some servants of the king were working as guards for an ox-cart to earn some extra pay. Towards nightfall, it so happened that the cart overturned for no apparent reason at a point that was two leagues away from the city on the southeast. Since they couldn't fix the cart that night, they decided to stay there until morning. Before long, a big crowd of people had collected around the cart. When morning came, and they were fixing the cart, they noticed that the rim of the cart's wheel had turned to pure gold. Without thinking of keeping that gold for themselves, they went straight to Kakati Prolaraju and told him what had happened. Filled with amazement, the king hurried to the spot together with his advisors, priests, and ministers, and there they discovered buried in the ground a touchstone *linga* of Sambhu. The king attempted to move that golden *linga* full of light to Hanumakonda, but that god would not budge. Kakati Prolaraju decided to summon Ramaranya Shripada and Mahendra Shripada who were residents of Kaleshvaram, and Tridandi Rishi who lived at the Hidimba Ashrama. He went out to greet them as they arrived, honoring them by giving them water to drink and water for washing their feet, and then he showed that god to them.

With great joy, the sages applied sacred ash to that god, and decided to construct a city one *yojana* in extent around it, so that the god would stand at its centre. Thus, in the 909th year of the Shalivahana-Shaka era, in the cyclic year Subhakrit, on Thursday, the fifth day of the bright fortnight of the month of Kartika, under the asterism of Rohini, they constructed the city of Warangal.

In order that the city should be invincible, Ramaranya Shripada decided to lay out the lines for the fort according to the *yantra* called Shrividyakramambu, and he had a boundary wall constructed around it.

They laid out a road two *krosas* long, running from the gate of Hanumakonda up to the temple of the touchstone *linga* of Shiva, and along both sides of it they constructed temples: 250 Shaiva temples, dedicated to the gods Muktishvara, Shri Vishvanatha, Bhimeshvara, Virupaksha, Rameshvara, and others; 100 Vaishnava temples dedicated to Venkatanatha, Shriranganayaka, Gopala, Panchalaraya, and other forms of Vishnu; 50 temples of the Goddess; and 40 temples dedicated to such deities as Virabhadra, Vinayaka, and Bhairava.

After consecrating these temples, Ramaranya Shripada turned to Kakati Prolaraja and said: 'Everyday, immediately after you worship Sambhulinga, touch some iron to his *linga* and it will become pure gold. Distribute that gold daily to brahmins.'

The king then asked Ramaranya Shripada to explain the system of weights and measures to him, and Ramaranya complied: 'Listen while I explain the rates of weights.' Ramaranya said: 'A weight of 120 *gurijas* is called one *tula*; 120 of those *tulas* are called one *vise;* and 120 of these *vises* are called one *baruva*. This is the *baruvu* in common use in the present Kali Age.' Once he had explained all this, Ramaranya Shripada took the king's permission to leave and departed for Kaleshvaram together with the other sages who had accompanied him.

Thereafter, with the permission of the sages, Kakati Prolaraju every day had a one-*baruva* weight of iron brought, and touched it to that radiant touchstone *linga*, whereupon it would turn into pure gold. And the king daily made a gift of that gold to the gods and brahmins for their own use. After some time, a son was born to the king.

No. 4: INSCRIPTION OF RUDRADEVA

This excerpt comes from the Hanamkonda Thousand-Pillared Temple inscription of 1163, (adapted from P. Sreenivasachar, Corpus of Inscriptions in the Telangana Districts II: 3).

Side I: "Om! Hail! May there be wealth, victory, and prosperity.

Hail! The prosperous Maha-mandaleshvara [great feudatory], the Kakatiya king Rudradeva, who has attained the five great sounds, who is a Maha-mandaleshvara, whose actions are for the good of his lord, to whom modesty was an ornament:

While he was ruling the victorious kingdom, increasing in prosperity from day to day as long as the moon, the sun, and the stars, in the city of Anmakonda, enjoying pleasing conversations;

In the Shaka year 1084 [1163 CE] being the present cyclic year Chitrabhanu, in the month of Magha, on the thirteenth day of the bright fortnight, Saturday, he established Rudreshvara, Shri-Vasudevara, and Shri-Suryadevara. .....

Side III: "He [Rudradeva] had a capital city named Anumakonda, which was like the capital of the goddess of fortune, raised to a great state by the rise of the excellent and full grace of the God Shiva who was there; which was full of delight like the city of the love god Kama; which had the display of the feelings of love like the city of Indra; which had Indra and Vishnu as images in its temples; and which was beautiful with the charm of plantain trees;

Where the women were indeed in the metropolis of the love god, having eyes like the petals of the blue lotuses and slim bodies, they were like ornaments to the women of the three worlds, and had bodies weighed down by the weight of big and high breasts;

Where in the houses of the excellent brahmins clever parrots join the students, though prevented, and study the Vedas, which contain all the Vedangas, all appropriate subjects, beautiful histories, and are in well-studied word order;

And where, in the houses of courtesans the loud and sweet sounds of young parrots make all the quarters resound – parrots imitating the sounds of amorous sports in sexual enjoyment, which are during day-time like full moons to the billowing ocean of the pride of the love of men about town."

Side IV: "His kingdom is up to the seashore on the East and extends always over the full South up to the mountain Shrishaila; on the West the prosperous kingdom continues as far as the neighborhood of Kataka, and in the North as far as the neighborhood of the mountain slopes of Malyavanta, shining in the Northern quarter.

King Rudradeva, respected by the good, gave as a permanent gift the great village named Maddicheruvula for the sake of services for Gods Shiva, Surya, and Vishnu."

No. 5: INSCRIPTION OF RECHERLA RUDRA

These excerpts come from the Palampet inscription of 1213 (from Inscriptions at Palampet and Uparpalli, Hyderabad Archaeological Series, No. 3*, Hyderabad, 1919).*

And this blest General Rudra, a man of skill, made a consecration of the god Rudreshvara in the city of Orugallu [Warangal]. And the sage son of Kamamba then granted to this Siva, for the accomplishment of enjoyment of theatrical performances and bodily pleasure, the village named Nekkonda.

By him was built a city brilliantly shooting up lofty pinnacles, in which are delightful palaces, constant fortunes of every kind. It is forever a blessed Dvaravati, an Ayodhya together with Girivraja and a blessed Vishala, and a Mathura manifestly, and a Bhogavati.

Here in one part is heard the sound of mighty roaring of towering lordly elephants, in another part the multitudinous clattering of the hard hoofs of squadrons of horses, in another, the sportive clamour of warlike exercises carried on by troops of warriors, in another the mutual altercation of numerous libertines in gambling companies;

In another part the sound of damsels' songs mingled with the sweetness of novel musical performances, in another the brilliance of goodly discourses by ardent students of the sciences. As if on purpose to behold the splendour of this city, the betel-creepers quickly climb up to the top of the shoulders of the areca-palms in the parks all around.

He constructed a pond, which stands like an ocean that has come thither from fear of the Submarine Fire, and looks like a mirror for that city. In this pond the banks, covered with rows of waves and underlined with foam all along the water-edge, suggest a resemblance to the ocean, being like in aspect to rows of shells of quivering lustre.

All the clouds certainly take up its water, not that of the ocean, for they everywhere carry sweet water. All the stainless stars in the nights, entering its exceedingly pure waters in the form of reflected images of themselves, ever freely perform in sooth the austerity of water-dwelling in order to be united with the full moon.

At this pond, which is loved by troops of birds delighted at the swinging play of the lines of gently rising, abundant, sportive, quivering waves, the *chataka* birds all around in the hot season drink the pure water-drops dashed up by the fishes' tails as they fall far away, imagining them to be rain.

In this exceedingly brilliant city this Rudra, who was a terror to rival warriors, performed a consecration of Rudreshvara, which was extolled by great brahmins. On the top of the temple of this god shines distinctly a golden cupola, illumining the space of the sky, always having the brilliance of a vast sun's orb standing on the lofty peak of the Eastern Mountain.

In the Shaka year numbered as "earth, moon, worlds, arrows" [=1135 Saka Era=1213 CE], the cyclic year Shrimukha, in the month Madhu, on the eighth day of the bright fortnight, a Sunday, and under the asterism Pushya, he, great of mind granted respectfully to Rudreshvara together with Gaurisha Upparlapalli and Borlapalli for their enjoyment.

Whether born of my lineage or born of the lineage of other kings, may monarchs on earth with minds free from sin maintain this my pious foundation in its entirety; to them I clasp my hands upon my head. Even though it be made by an enemy, a religious foundation should be maintained with care; for an enemy will be merely an enemy, but a religious foundation can be an enemy to no man.

He who should take away land, whether granted by himself or granted by others, is born for 60,000 years as a worm in dung.

Therefore, O kings, you must carefully maintain with affection the religious foundation made by us, in order that your welfare may increase.

The blest General Rudra, the sage, rejoicing granted to the god who is well established in the ever-fortunate goodly town of Atukuru, to Katesvara and to Kamesvara and Rudresvara, the excellent village of Nradkude for their enjoyment.

LIST OF KAKATIYA RULERS

Prola II (1116-57)
Rudradeva (1157-95)
Mahadeva (1195-98)
Ganapatideva (1199-1262)
Rudramadevi (1262-89)
Prataparudra (1289-1323)

Palampet, Ramappa Temple, carved relief of dancers and musicians

GLOSSARY

This list is mostly of Indian terms and names.

asthana-mandapa, "court hall", a distinctive type of pillared hall, defining the southern entrance to a royal temple complex

Atukuru, Kakatiya-period name of Palampet

Balarama, elder brother of Krishna and avatar of Vishnu's snake Shesha

bund, dam wall constructed to make a water reservoir (*cheruvu*)

chaubara, "four-fold house", a monument marking a city center at the crossing of its four main avenues

cheruvu, a man-made water reservoir

Betana, a minister of Kakatiya Prola II

Bhumija, one of the "public" modes used in Kakatiya temple architecture, in which each projection of the wall is moulded as a single, broad pilaster

chatur-mukha linga, a ***linga*** with four faces of Siva projecting from the shaft

devalayam, "residence of a god", a common term for a temple

Dharanendra, the male protective deity of the Jain savior Parshvanatha

Durga, active and violent form of the goddess who slayed the water-buffalo demon

Gajalakshmi, a form of the goddess of wealth and prosperity, Lakshmi, flanked by two elephants lustrating her with water

Gajasura, an elephant demon slain by Shiva

Ganesha, the elephant-headed god who removes obstacles; one of Shiva's sons

Gaurisha, Shiva as Lord of his consort, the goddess Gauri

girih, "knot" in Persian, name given to a type of Islamic ornament consisting of stars formed by interlacing strapwork

gudi, Telugu word for temple

Jambudvipa, the circular, rose-apple continent occupying the center of the inhabited universe according to Hindu cosmology

Kadalalaya Basadi, name of a Jain temple in Hanamkonda established in 1117 through the patronage of Mailama, the wife of Kakatiya Prola II's minister Betana

Kakati, a local goddess, adopted as the tutelary deity of the Kakatiya dynasty

Kaliya, serpent demon subdued by Krishna who danced on his hoods

kalyana-mandapa, type of pillared hall where the yearly wedding of a temple's god and goddess is performed

kirtimukha, a decorative monster mask

kirti-torana, "portal of glory", term used for the ceremonial portals of the Svayambhu Shiva temple in Warangal

Krishna, flute-playing, cowherd avatar of Vishnu

Lakshmana, younger brother of Rama, an avatar of Vishnu

linga, the god Shiva in the form of a phallic emblem

Madhava Varman, legendary founder of the Kakatiya dynasty

Mailama, wife of Kakatiya Prola II's minister Betana; founder of the Kadalalaya Basadi in Hanamkonda

makara, aquatic monster with crocodile jaws and a florid, vegetal tail

makara-torana, decorative arch, often found at the entrance to temple vestibules, taking the form of an undulating vegetal scroll emerging from the mouths of a pair of *makara* crocodiles

mandapa, pillared hall for worshippers; can be either attached to or detached from the temple proper

Meru, name of the cosmic mountain rising up from the center of Jambudvipa according to Hindu cosmology

mihrab, in Islamic architecture, the arched niche in the back wall of a mosque or similar structure; commemorates the place taken by the Prophet Muhammad during prayer

minbar, in Islamic architecture, refers to a stepped pulpit placed against the back wall of a congregational mosque, from which special prayers are offered on behalf of the ruler and the community, at the time of the Friday noon prayer

Nagara, North Indian tradition of temple architecture, characterized by the curvilinear profile of the spire over its sanctum

Narasimha, Man-Lion incarnation of Vishnu, who slayed the demon Hiranyakashipu

Nandi, bull mount of Shiva; in Shiva temples, his image is often placed in a separate pavilion on axis with his master's image inside the temple

Neminatha, the 22nd Jain Tirthankara

Padmakshi, the Hindu goddess worshipped at Hanamkonda as the consort of Siddheshvara; was originally the Jain deity Padmavati

Padmavati, protective goddess of the Jain Tirthankara Parshvanatha

Panchaliraya, name of Vishnu as worshipped by the epic heroine Draupadi (also known as Panchali)

Parshvanatha, the 23rd Jain Tirthankara

Parvati, peaceful aspect of the goddess, in the form of Shiva's consort

Phamsana, "private" mode used in Kakatiya temple architecture, in which the walls are treated as a plain, masonry surface without any articulation

Polavasa-desha, Kakatiya period name for the region around Palampet and Ghanpur

Prataparudra Charitramu, popular Telugu prose account of the Kakatiya dynasty, written in Warangal by Ekamranatha c. 1550

qibla, the direction from any location toward Mecca, which Muslims face during ritual prayer; in Telangana this is approximately west or just north of west

Rama, one of Vishnu's avatars

ranga-mandapa, "stage pavilion", the most common mandapa type in Kakatiya architecture, consisting of nine bays in a 3 by 3 grid, with the central bay occupied by a raised circular platform providing a stage for dance performances for the deity

Sahasralinga Ganapatishvara, name of a temple in Warangal dedicated to Siva in the form of a thousand-shafted *linga*, and named after Kakatiya Ganapatideva

Sarasvati, goddess of learning, poetry, and the arts

Sarvatobhadra, "auspicious on all sides"; a special type of temple with doors opening on all four sides of the central shrine

Shambhunigudi, the small Siva temple complex located just to the south of the Svayambhu Shiva temple precinct in Warangal

Shantinatha, the 16th Jain Tirthankara

siddha, in a Hindu context, a perfected yogi who has attained magical powers; in a Jain context, a fully liberated soul

Siddheshvara, form of Shiva worshipped in Hanamkonda as lord of the *siddhas*.

Siddheshvara Charitramu, "The story of Siddhesvara", a 17th-century Telugu account of how Siddhesvara manifested at Hanamkonda; the work is an expanded version in verse of the *Prataparudra Charitramu*

Sita, the wife of Rama

Shiva, one of the primary gods of Hinduism; associated with asceticism, creation and destruction

Surya, the Sun god in Hinduism

Svayambhu Shiva, "The Self-Manifest Shiva", the form of Shiva worshipped at the center of Warangal who was the state deity of the Kakatiyas since the late 12th century

Tirthankara, "Maker of a Crossing", a great teacher of the Jain religion, of whom the Jains count 24, the most recent one being the historical Mahavira, a contemporary of the Buddha

trikuta, "three-peaked", a common type of temple in Telangana, with three towered shrines, one opening on to each of three sides of a common *mandapa*, with the entrance porch on the fourth

Tripurushas, "The Three Beings", the three gods Shiva, Vishnu, and Surya, worshipped together as a triad in a *trikuta* temple

Venkateshvara temple, popular name of a temple in Warangal Fort that was constructed in the early 16th century out of Kakatiya components and was dedicated to the worship of Panchaliraya, a form of Krishna

Vesara, a "public" mode used in Kakatiya temple architecture, in which each projection of the wall is articulated by a pair of slender pilasters at its edges

Vishnu, one of the great gods of Hinduism, associated with preservation of the cosmic and social order

yali, a mythical beast or leogryph, usually of leonine form with horns and aspects of other beasts

FURTHER READING

Barnett, L.D. *Inscriptions at Palampet and Uparpalli*, Hyderabad Archaeological Series, no. 3, Hyderabad, 1919.

Dhaky, M.A. *Encyclopaedia of Indian Temple Architecture: South India, Upper Dravidadesa, Later Phase, AD 973-1326.* New Delhi, American Institute of Indian Studies, 1996.

Eaton, Richard M. *A Social History of the Deccan, 1300-1761: Eight Indian Lives.* Cambridge, Cambridge University Press, 2005.

Eaton, Richard M. and Phillip B. Wagoner. *Power, Memory, Architecture: Contested Sites on India's Deccan Plateau, 1300-1600.* New Delhi, Oxford University Press, 2014.

Gopalakrishna Murthy, S. *The Sculpture of the Kakatiyas*. Hyderabad, Government of Andhra Pradesh, 1964.

Hirananda Sastri. *Shitab Khan of Warangal.* Hyderabad Archaeological Series, no. 9. Hyderabad, Nizam's Government, 1932

Michell, George, "City as Cosmogram: The Circular Plan of Warangal." *South Asian Studies*, 8 (1992): 1-18.

Narayana Rao, V. and David Shulman. *A Lover's Guide to Warangal: The Kridabhiramamu of Vinukonda Vallabharaya.* New Delhi, Permanent Black, 2002.

Pandu Ranga Rao, M., ed. *Engineering and Technological Achievements during the Kakatiya Period.* Warangal, INTACH, 1996.

Parabrahma Sastry, P.V. *The Kakatiyas of Warangal*. Hyderabad, Government of Andhra Pradesh, 1978.

Radhakrishna Sarma, M. *Temples of Telingana*. Hyderabad, 1972.

Ramachandra Murthy, N.S. *Forts of Andhra Pradesh (from the earliest times up to 16th C. AD)*. Delhi, Bharatiya Kala Prakashan, 1996.

Ramanaiah, J. *Temples of South India: A Study of Hindu, Jain, and Buddhist Monuments of the Deccan [Karimnagar District]*. New Delhi, Concept Publishing, 1989.

Sreenivasachar, P. *A Corpus of Inscriptions in the Telingana Districts of H.E.H. The Nizam's Dominions*, Hyderabad Archaeological Series, no. 13. Hyderabad, Nizam's Government, 1940.

Talbot, Cynthia. *Precolonial India in Practice: Society, Region, and Identity in Medieval Andhra.* New York, Oxford University Press, 2001.

– . "Rudrama-devi, the Female King: Gender and Political Authority in Medieval India." In David Shulman, ed. *Syllables of Sky: Studies in South Indian Civilization in Honour of Velcheru Narayana Rao*. Delhi, Oxford University Press, 1995. Pp. 391-430.

Venkataramanayya, N. *Inscriptions of Andhra Pradesh: Warangal District.* Hyderabad, Government of Andhra Pradesh, 1974.

Wagoner, Phillip B. "A Dense Epitome of the World: The Image of Warangal in the *Kridabhiramamu*." Afterword to Velcheru Narayana Rao and David Shulman, trans. *A Lover's Guide to Warangal: The*

Kridabhiramamu of Vinukonda Vallabharaya. New Delhi, Permanent Black, 2002. Pp. 85-103

–. "KOS MAHAL," *Encyclopædia Iranica*, online edition, 2017, available at http://www.iranicaonline.org/articles/khosh-mahal (30 May 2017).

–. "Modal Marking of Temple Types in Kakatiya Andhra: Towards a Theory of Decorum for Indian Temple Architecture." In David Shulman, ed. *Syllables of Sky: Studies in South Indian Civilization in Honour of Velcheru Narayana Rao.* Delhi: Oxford University Press, 1995. Pp. 431-72.

Wagoner, Phillip B. and John Henry Rice. "From Delhi to the Deccan: Newly Discovered Tughluq Monuments at Warangal-Sultanpur and the Beginnings of Indo-Islamic Architecture in Southern India." *Artibus Asiae*, 61/1 (2001): 77-117.

Yazdani, Ghulam. *The Temples at Palampet.* Memoirs of the Archaeological Survey of India, No.6. Calcutta, 1922.

INDEX

Page numbers in **colour** have illustrations